GOODBYE DEPRESSION

(Overcome depression with my two-way strategies within 21 days)

OLAMITI BUSAYO IMOLEAYO

DEDICATION

This book is dedicated to God Almighty; my reality, my life, and the lifter of my head. My life was transformed amazingly when I met Him. Thank you precious Holy Spirit. This book is specially dedicated to everyone battling with depression out there, be aware you are not alone. help is here. Amen

CONTENTS

ACKNOWLEDGMENTS

I have found grace and favor from the Lord, and this has been the reason I was blessed not only with parents but also with counselors. My heartfelt appreciation always goes to you, Dad and Mum, for your love and passion, which is helping me become a meaningful person in life. Thank you, Dad and Mum.

I have discovered that having siblings is not just a blessing; having ones who truly care and can journey with you even in trying times is priceless. To all my siblings, thank you for your unconditional love. The Lord is your reward.

To my spiritual parents, Pastor and Pastor Mrs. Christopher Akinola, Daddy, and Mummy, I owe you a great deal. My pastor and friend, Papa Praise Chukwuemeka thanks for your sacrifice, dear friend.

It would be ungrateful not to acknowledge these special people for their counsel and support: Pastor and Mrs. Rotimi Emmanuel, Hon. Omoloye Ilesanmi, Mr. Adeduyite Olaleye, Mr. Irerisola, Mummy Praise Babs thank you, lovers of God, Dr. Olusanya Oyewole, thank you sir for sacrificing your precious time to proofread this work, Mr. Akindoyin Oluwadare, Mr. Seun, Jay success Tv thanks brotherly. I celebrate and appreciate you all.

To my editor, Mr. Paul Ajibo, Sir, your passion for helping me become a better version of myself, even when times are tough, is commendable. You dedicated the most crucial part of your time to editing this work. Thank you, sir. More blessings I pray.

To my motivators, the people who see greatness in me and have been the fuel in my car: Esther Ibifaka, Destiny Epoagba, Emmanuel, Julius Ibukun, Papa Sammy, Mama Dorcas Oluwatosin, Samuel, Racheal and Mercy. Please accept my sincere appreciation. Special thanks to my crew. I want you all to know that without you, there would be no "The Light." Thanks for always showing up. I acknowledge my baby girls, Oluwasemilore Emmanuel and Adesewa. Sweetheart, Uncle loves you big. Thanks for your sincere love.

Lastly, I owe you a lot to everyone who has been supporting this vision in one way or another. I pray the Lord rewards you abundantly. Much love from,

Busayo Imoleayo

The Light

FORWARD

Imagine losing your wife just 14 days after a big wedding ceremony, taken away by the cold hand of death. What could depress a man beyond that? However, I knew I could not succumb to depression without a fight. Many people came around brethren, family, and friends trying to rally around me and ensure I did not fall into despair. Ironically, their presence alone sometimes felt suffocating, pushing me closer to the edge. So, as much as possible, I avoided them. And today, I can confidently say I never succumbed to depression.

How was I able to achieve this? That is one of the reasons why this book, **Goodbye Depression**, is essential for you to read. Some of the lessons I learned before my trial, which helped me navigate through the darkest days, are discussed in this book. Whether you are currently struggling with depression or maintaining your mental health, this book is for you. Life has seasons for everyone today might be rosy and filled with smiles, but a time may come when life will test you with its harshness.

Busayo Imoleayo, a devoted Christian who authored this book, has faced immense challenges in his own life. His journey is a testament to resilience, faith, and the power of divine guidance. As you turn the pages of this book, you will see the diligence and effort he has put into this work. He has meticulously explored the depths of depression and the paths to overcoming it, offering readers a lifeline drawn from his own experiences and profound faith and research.

I am certain that the Holy Spirit inspired this work. The wisdom and insights contained within these pages are not just the product of human effort but are imbued with divine inspiration. Busayo's faith and reliance on God's guidance shine through, making this book a beacon of hope for anyone facing mental health challenges.

In Goodbye Depression, you will find practical advice, spiritual encouragement, and a roadmap to navigate life's toughest seasons. Equip yourself with the tools to face whatever life throws your way, knowing that you are not alone and that there is a path to overcoming even the darkest of times.

Irerinsola.

RCCG, Ondo Province 15 Youth President.

INTRODUCTION

Depression is more than just a fleeting feeling of sadness; it's a complex and exhausting mental health condition that affects millions of people worldwide. From the depths of hopelessness to the shadows that seem to linger, depression casts a heavy burden on individuals, families, and communities. Its prevalence is astonishing, with statistics painting a clear picture of its reach. Yet, behind every statistic lies a story of struggle, resilience, and the quest for healing. In this book, "Goodbye Depression," Busayo delves into the heart of this issue, shedding light on its prevalence and impact, and offering guidance, hope, and proven solutions through his two-way integrative approach to those who find themselves in its grip.

As someone who has walked the winding path of depression, and has developed deep feelings for those who are currently treading the path, I understand firsthand the weight it carries and the toll it takes on every aspect of life. The silent battles fought within, the moments of despair that seem endless, and the search for a twinkle of light in the darkness is all too familiar when the world has turned upside down and everything seems to be over. I've seen loved ones struggle with their demons, their pain echoing mine. These personal experiences have fueled my passion to reach out, to connect, and to offer a beacon of hope to those who may feel lost in the web of depression.

In "Goodbye Depression," we embark on a journey of understanding, healing, and transformation. This book serves as a comprehensive guide, bringing insights, strategies, and practical tools from science and faith to navigate the dark path of depression. From unraveling the threads of its causes to discovering the pathways to recovery through what I call the diamond and golden approaches, caregivers and friends seeking support for loved ones are not left behind. This book offers valuable resources, actionable steps, and a roadmap toward saying goodbye to depression and embracing a life of renewed hope and vitality.

MY MODEL

Man is comprised of two components: dust and spirit. Our survival hinges on these two elements. Similarly, our intake of information is divided between these components. Everything we absorb is stored in our minds, which serve as a balancing point for both the body and spirit. If one's existence is solely based on the body or flesh, rationalizing everything through a physical lens, the mind will only comprehend and develop in alignment with the flesh. This is why many esteemed professors or scientists struggle to grasp spiritual concepts.

Conversely, an individual who lives solely by the spirit, neglecting formal education or worldly knowledge, and relying solely on biblical teachings and divine revelations, may excel spiritually but struggle in worldly matters. The former can be likened to a person solely consuming physical food for growth, neglecting spiritual nourishment. The latter resembles someone who sustains solely on spiritual food, neglecting physical sustenance. Just as the person who forsakes physical food cannot survive, nor can the one who disregards spiritual matters survive.

As long as we inhabit this earth, we will always require these two components for our existence. Thus, God is deeply concerned about our wellbeing, which is why He designed this system for our sustenance.

In light of this revelation, I have developed an integrative model to address depressive disorder or depression, incorporating both scientific and faith-based approaches. I encourage you not to overlook either approach, whether it be the medical, social, or faith-based aspect. Adopting both methods will accelerate your recovery. My primary goal is to restore your hope and joy, allowing you to live the remainder of your life in peace and total rest.

2 Thessalonians 3:16 (KJV): "Now the Lord of peace himself give you peace always by all means. The Lord be with you all. Amen."

PART 1
THE MYTH OF DEPRESSION

CHAPTER 1

UNDERSTANDING DEPRESSION

Success felt like a dark cloud followed her everywhere after the loss of her mother. Her hobby was drawing and painting because she had a passion for art. Currently, her interest is lost in what she once delighted in. Every day was a struggle to find a reason to smile. One day, she found a dusty gallery hidden in her room. As she flipped through its pages, she saw beautiful images painted by her. With each flip of a page, a glimmer of hope emerged. Success realized that even in the darkest times, there were moments of light waiting to be discovered. She decided to reach out to a friend she hadn't spoken to in a while after discovering her picture in the art album. The simple act of talking lifted a weight off her chest. Slowly, she began to open up, to share her struggles with someone who cared. Though the road to recovery was long, Success knew she had taken the first step. With each day, she found a little more strength, and a little more courage to face the world. As she decided to engage in what she loved doing, her joy was restored, and then she realized that no storm could ever truly extinguish her light.

Truly no storm could ever extinguish your light as you've decided to take a walk with me as we both journey through the pages of this book titled Goodbye Depression. With me promising you and crossing my heart that before you read till the end, you will have every cause to smile and you will be healed, whole, and transformed. Are you ready? Let's go.

Now, let's quickly dive into the meaning of the word Depression.

Definition of Depression

Depressive disorder, also known as depression, is not simply feeling down or sad; it's a complex mental health disorder that affects how you think, feel, and handle daily activities. Common misconceptions lead people to label depression as a sign of weakness or just a passing phase that will fade with time. No, it's not, and it won't. However, depression is a legitimate medical condition that requires understanding and support. It's crucial to do away with these myths and recognize depression for what it truly is: a serious illness that can impact anyone, regardless of age, gender, background, and economic status.

While the exact causes of depression remain unknown, it's believed to result from a combination of genetic, biological, environmental, psychological, and spiritual factors. Imbalances in brain chemicals, such as serotonin and dopamine, play a significant role in regulating mood and emotions. Traumatic life events, chronic stress, medical conditions, certain medications, and other factors can also contribute to the development of depression. Understanding these factors can help individuals and loved ones navigate the complexities of depression and seek appropriate support and treatment.

Bethany Juby, an American psychologist (October 2023), indicates that depression ranks among the most widespread mental health conditions globally. According to the World Health Organization (WHO), over 280 million individuals of all age groups suffer from depression worldwide. This statistic accounts for approximately 5% of the global population, with 4% affecting men and 6% affecting women, and a prevalence of 5.7% among adults aged over 60.

In Nigeria, depression affects an estimated 50% of the population, with a higher incidence observed among women compared to men, particularly among those in the lower and middle-income class. The populace in Nigeria exhibits a lack of sufficient understanding concerning mental health disorders and harbors various misconceptions regarding their root causes, such as substance abuse (drug abuse) (80.8%), demonic possession (30.2%), traumatic experiences or shock (29.9%), stress (29.2%), and genetic inheritance (26.5%). A minority attribute these disorders to biological factors or brain diseases. These insights were drawn from a study published on PubMed Central on March 31, 2023. Let's delve into the symptoms of depressive disorder or depression.

Symptoms of Depressive Disorder or Depression

There are several symptoms of depression. Psychologists have helped us to narrow them down to the ones I will outline below. If you experience some of the following signs and symptoms nearly every day for at least 2 weeks, you may be living with depression. These symptoms include:

1. Feeling sad, anxious, or "empty"

2. Feeling hopeless, worthless, and pessimistic

3. Crying a lot

4. Feeling bothered, annoyed, or angry

5. Loss of interest in hobbies and interests you once enjoyed

6. Decreased energy or fatigue

7. Difficulty concentrating, remembering, or making decisions

8. Moving or talking more slowly

9. Difficulty sleeping, early morning awakening, or oversleeping

10. Appetite or weight changes, such as eating too much or eating less

11. Chronic physical pain with no clear cause that does not get better with treatment (headaches, aches or pains, digestive problems, cramps)
12. Thoughts of death, suicide, self-harm, or suicide attempts. This is very common; almost everyone is familiar with this.

Now, what are the types of depression?

Types of depression according to mental health practitioners

1. Clinical depression (major depressive disorder)

2. Persistent depressive disorder (PDD)

3. Disruptive mood dysregulation disorder (DMDD)

4. Premenstrual dysphoric disorder (PMDD)

5. Depressive disorder due to another medical condition

6. Seasonal affective disorder (seasonal depression)

7. Prenatal depression and postpartum depression

1.   Clinical depression (major depressive disorder): A diagnosis of major depressive disorder means you've felt sad, low, or worthless most days for at least two weeks while also having other symptoms such as sleep problems, loss of interest in activities, or change in appetite. This is the most severe form of depression and one of the most common forms.

2.   Persistent depressive disorder (PDD): Persistent depressive disorder is mild or moderate depression that lasts for at least two years. The symptoms are less severe than major depressive disorder. Healthcare providers used to call PDD dysthymia.

3. **Disruptive mood dysregulation disorder (DMDD):** DMDD causes chronic, intense irritability and frequent anger outbursts in children. Symptoms usually begin by the age of 10.

4. **Premenstrual dysphoric disorder (PMDD):** With PMDD, you have premenstrual syndrome (PMS) symptoms along with mood symptoms, such as extreme irritability, anxiety, or depression. This type of Depression is found among women. It usually develops a few days before their monthly period and improves within a few days after their period starts, but it can be severe enough to interfere with your life.

5. **Depressive disorder due to another medical condition:** Many medical conditions can create changes in your body that cause depression. Examples include heart disease, HIV/AIDS, cancer, etc. If you're able to treat the underlying condition, the depression usually improves as well.

6. **Seasonal affective disorder (seasonal depression):** This is a form of major depressive disorder that typically arises during the fall and winter and goes away during the spring and summer.

7. **Prenatal depression and postpartum depression:** Prenatal depression is depression that happens during pregnancy. It's a form of Depression experienced among pregnant woman that normally affects their mood such as extreme fear or hopelessness. While Postpartum depression is depression that develops within four weeks of delivering a baby, this likely arises as a fear of being a mother.

In the next chapter, we shall be exploring the cause of Depression according to health practitioners and researchers don't give up (smile) let's go

CHAPTER 2

THE CAUSES OF DEPRESSION

Depression is a complex mental health condition influenced by several factors, both internal and external. Understanding the root causes is crucial for effectively managing and overcoming depression.

NOTE: Researchers don't know the exact cause of depression. They think that several factors contribute to its development, including:

1. Brain chemistry: An imbalance of neurotransmitters, including serotonin and dopamine, contributes to the development of depression.
2. Medical conditions: Chronic pain and chronic conditions like diabetes, heart disease, cancer, and other incurable diseases can lead to depression.
3. Medication: Some medications can cause depression as a side effect due to their abuse. Substance use, including alcohol, marijuana, cocaine, heroin, and inhalants (glue, paint, thinner), can also cause depression or make it worse.
4. Family history: You're at a higher risk for developing depression if you have a family history of depression or another mood disorder.

5. Early childhood trauma: Some events affect the way your body reacts to fear and stressful situations due to traumatic events you've encountered while growing up.

To have an elaborate knowledge about the topic, I delved deep into the space to gather more factors from social science researchers, and these are the notable factors:

1. Biological Factors: Biological predispositions, such as genetics and neurochemical imbalances, can contribute to the development of depression. Research suggests that individuals with a family history of depression may be at higher risk due to inherited genetic vulnerabilities. Additionally, alterations in neurotransmitters, such as serotonin, dopamine, and norepinephrine, play a role in regulating mood and emotions.

2. Environmental Triggers: Environmental pressures, such as traumatic life events, chronic stress, interpersonal conflicts, and socioeconomic challenges, can trigger or worsen depression. In Nigeria, factors such as poverty, unemployment, workplace pressure, political instability, and cultural stigma surrounding mental illness can contribute to feelings of hopelessness and despair. People living in Lagos will tend to understand this better because the rates of homelessness, work pressure, transportation pressure, and challenges in meeting basic needs are very high.

3. Psychological Factors: Psychological vulnerabilities, including low self-esteem (I once suffered from this; how I overcame it will be shared in a subsequent chapter), perfectionism (this relates to the melancholic temperament), and negative thinking patterns, can increase susceptibility to depression. In Nigeria, cultural expectations, gender roles, and societal pressures may influence individuals' perceptions of themselves and their ability to cope with pressures.

4. Social Determinants: Social factors, such as social isolation, lack of social support, and discrimination, can significantly impact mental health. In Nigeria, societal norms and attitudes towards mental illness may discourage individuals from seeking help or

disclosing their struggles, leading to feelings of isolation and shame. This implies that the way Nigerians perceive people living with mental illness has led to a reluctance to seek help, even when they are perfectly healed.

Furthermore, while various writers and researchers have identified several factors, I aim to focus solely on the aforementioned ones. Additionally, I will unveil other factors I have discovered over time, which I refer to as 'Stressful life events.' I look forward to delving into these in the next chapter.

CHAPTER 3

STRESSFUL LIFE EVENTS

In this chapter of Goodbye Depression, we shall be looking at Stressful life events. Which I defined as significant occurrences or circumstances that interrupt one's emotional stability, potentially leading to increased levels of stress and contributing to the development of hopelessness. The stressful life events have discovered over time are as follows

1. **The Loss of a Loved One:** Our connection with those we cherish transcends mere physical presence, extending into the depths of our souls. Many among us have endured the heartbreaking departure of cherished individuals be it both parents, a mother, a father, a spouse, siblings, or others. Each loss carves a profound void and invites the specter of depression. Please accept my heartfelt condolences.

I implore you to recognize that countless individuals have grappled with similar grief, and many continue to navigate its depths to this day. I understand the depth of your affection for him/her, and the solemn vows you made to honor your love for him/her.

While yours might be either of your parents or both, I understand that the love between a parent and child transcends words; the promise to care for them is inscribed in the very fabric of our beings. Yet, despite our best intentions, death cruelly snatches them away from us. Deeply sorry about that.

For you, the anguish of navigating life's pathways without the guidance of a loved one looms large in your heart. Perhaps thoughts of how to proceed as a student now cloud your mind, with promises of educational support from daddy or mummy, which had become fiction. I empathize with your plight, and I am here not to dwell or remind you of the past, but to offer solace and reignite the flames of hope.

I, too, have endured the loss of a dear family friend a man who held a special place in my heart, though not a direct parent. For a prolonged period, grief held me in its grip, mirroring the journey of the young lady whose story graced the opening of this book called 'SUCCESS.' So, how did I find healing? How did I rediscover hope? I shall reveal every detail, leaving no stone unturned in the pages that follow.

2. **Economic Hardship:** In the face of economic instability, unemployment, and post-graduation frustration, it's natural to feel overwhelmed. As a family man, the pressure to provide for your family amidst Nigeria's economic challenges can be daunting. As your job becomes outdated and financial obligations mount, it's easy to twist into hopelessness. Remember, survival in Nigeria often depends on Grace rather than grade. Take a moment to breathe. While it may seem like there's no way out, I've come to inform you there's hope. Here is a brief history of my family.

A few years ago, my family was immersed in abject poverty. We struggled to find enough food to eat, lacked decent clothing, and felt like we had no direction in life. Every meal was a challenge. But today, the story has changed. Despite the ongoing economic frustrations in our nation, we have managed to improve our situation to some extent. We are grateful for the progress we've made.

My advice is that instead of dwelling on the problem, turn to resources that can pave the way for your growth. Consider the story of Harland Sanders, the visionary behind KFC, who faced setbacks before achieving success. Let his comeback inspire your journey. Start by focusing on small steps and leveraging available opportunities. You're not alone in this struggle, and with determination and resourcefulness, you will overcome.

3. Health Challenges: Millions of individuals grapple with health issues that not only affect their physical well-being but also take a toll on their mental health. Examples are those battling diseases such as cancer or HIV/AIDS, despite taking necessary precautions, who find themselves overwhelmed by depression. Additionally, there are health concerns that carry a stigma, making it difficult to discuss openly, such as adult bed-wetting and epilepsy. However, amidst these challenges, there is hope. Through my comprehensive approach, I've witnessed solutions to these issues firsthand. Recently, I encountered a woman diagnosed with brain cancer. While her husband was devastated, she remained remarkably composed, even challenging the diagnosis (Doctor). Despite the grim reality, she triumphed over cancer using one of the methods outlined in my approach. So, stay tuned and delve into this book to uncover valuable insights and strategies for overcoming health obstacles.

4. Conflict and Violence: Failed marriages, sexual harassment, child abuse, and domestic violence are significant contributors to depression. Many struggle to cope with the stress resulting from such situations, while some adapt to thrive in conflict. If you're experiencing depression, it may be linked to conflict and violence in your workplace, marriage, or surroundings. Are you facing similar challenges in your organization, neighborhood, or environment? I understand your struggle and can guide you towards resolution and restoring peace.

5. Family Challenges: Tensions within families, such as domestic violence or marital discord, are prevalent causes of depression. These issues often lead individuals to seek solace elsewhere, contributing to their emotional distress. Additionally, unstable family dynamics can drive youth towards negative influences and behaviors. Despite the difficulties, I've been thinking of ways to support you from the start.

6. Educational Pressures: The burden of high expectations in education, compounded by limited resources, has paved a path to depression for thousands of students in Nigeria and globally. During my first year of school, our tuition fee was a manageable 26,000 naira. However, with the arrival of a new governor in my state, the welcome message to my school was a staggering increase in tuition fees, soaring from 26,000 to 150,000 naira, with some departments paying even more. This sudden escalation bred frustration, driving many students into criminal activities, and desperation for quick fixes like hookup culture, cybercrime, or forced dropouts. Several of my peers, despite their intelligence and dedication, remain unable to graduate due to financial constraints. My graduation was a testament to divine grace, even from a low-income background.

7. **Urbanization Challenges:** The rapid pace of urbanization often results in severed ties to traditional support systems, exacerbating feelings of isolation and loneliness. This trend is particularly prevalent in urban areas, where familial bonds weaken as parents struggle to provide for their families, often working long hours with minimal interaction with their children. Spouses find themselves distant, and children yearn for parental attention. The solution to this pervasive issue lies within the pages of this book, offering insights to bridge the gap and foster healthier familial connections. Keep reading to discover actionable strategies.

8. **Unforgiveness:** The weight of unforgiveness has driven countless individuals into the depths of depression, some tragically resorting to suicide. Perhaps you've experienced a profound betrayal or offense that has left you swearing never to forgive or forget. Yet, as the saying goes, 'You won't know how powerful forgiveness is until you have something to forgive.' Letting go can be incredibly challenging, but holding onto resentment ties you firmly to the past, preventing any movement forward into the future. There are two types of unforgiveness:

- Unforgiveness for self
- Unforgiveness for others

Ask yourself: How long will you continue to imprison yourself? Holding onto grievances and self-blame only worsens the situation. Unforgiveness not only steals your present joy but also robs you of future possibilities. I've walked in your shoes and felt the pain firsthand.

Here's a method I've found effective in overcoming unforgiveness, both towards myself and others: I close my eyes, extend my hands forward, and fold them, recalling the hurtful scenario vividly through my inner mind. Sometimes tears accompany this process. Then, I call my name, or the name of the person involved, declaring 'I forgive you' and release my folded hand gradually, repeating it thrice. The relief that follows is indescribable, a weight lifted from my heart, and joy will flourish in my heart. Give it a try, it works faster than anything you can think of.

9. Depression as a result of non-access to phone and computer gadgets:

Through my research, I've found that many individuals are battling with depression due to non-access to phones and computer gadgets, often stemming from various factors such as power outages, particularly prevalent in places like Nigeria.

Kindly permit me to ask you this question: How will you feel if your phone is taken from you for 2 hours? Your answer is directly proportional to how likely you can fall into depression if not properly managed. In such cases like this, the inability to use phones can increase health issues like high blood pressure, especially among youth. My focus isn't primarily on individuals who rely on phones for business purposes; hence, it's crucial to note that many young people are heavily addicted to platforms like YouTube, TikTok, and other social media platforms. Hence depriving them from these platforms increases their heart pressure, leading to a sense of hopelessness and despair. As a writer, I suggest we learn phone management skills learn how to do away with our gadgets sometimes, and be free with people around us. However, beyond the factors we've discussed, there's another crucial factor contributing to depression that we cannot overlook. Are you tired? Let's not falter; instead, let's delve deeper and explore these contributing factors together.

CHAPTER 4

FEAR AND DEPRESSION

Fear is a result of emotion, and when you let your emotions control you instead of thinking logically, it becomes hard to make wise decisions. Many people are dominated by their emotions, affecting all areas of their lives. In this chapter,
I'll explore fear with the help of motivated examples and references from the scriptures.

Fear has its acronym to be

F- False

E- Events

A- Appearing

R- Real.

Tim LaHaye defines Fear as the paralyzing feelings of love, confidence, and well-being, it triggers negative thought patterns, breeding anxiety, and worry.

My definition of fear is the emotional response to information, ideas, stereotypes, and experiences that create a mental image that prevents action.

Our lives are influenced by what we see and hear, as well as the factors discussed in Chapter 3 of this book, with fear being directly connected to depression. Events that cause fear, which I refer to as fear-inducing events, make it difficult to heal oneself. The scriptural example of Adam's disobedience leading to fear supports this idea.

Genesis.3.10 He said, I heard the sound of You [walking] in the garden, and I was afraid because I was naked; and I hid myself. (AMP)

Sin is a crucial factor that induces fear. Other examples of fear-inducing events include sexual harassment, child abuse, domestic violence, loss of loved ones, Heartbroken, traumatic experiences, fear of what we become, and fear of the future. Understanding the link between fear and depression requires examining the effects of fear.

1.   Fear is often driven by emotions rather than rational thinking: Many individuals experience feelings of depression due to the state of their hearts, feeling lonely despite being surrounded by supportive individuals who genuinely care for them. This fear often stems from an excessive focus on security, leading to concerns about accidents or harm. Consequently, they become hesitant to engage with colleagues, neighbors, relatives, or even attend church. They prefer to isolate themselves as a precaution against potential evils, disregarding the fact that most of their fears are mere products of their imagination. These apprehensions arise from the information they consume or past experiences, without considering that just because something happened to someone else does not mean it will happen to them.

Moreover, some people drastically alter their nutrition habits based on a three-minute video. For instance, a man who typically enjoys pounded yam as his favorite meal stopped eating it after stumbling upon a video on Facebook that warned against elderly individuals consuming this dish. Similarly, social media has caused harm to numerous individuals creating mental images that induce fear.

Lastly, the fear of the coronavirus still lingers in some people's minds, leading them to maintain social distancing and be cautious about physical contact. Their precautions weren't based on not contracting the virus, but the fear within them that has encapsulated their heart, which continues to shape their behavior and choices.

2. **Fear as a result of individual temperament:** According to research, individuals with a melancholy or phlegmatic temperament tend to be more prone to constant fear than sanguine and choleric temperament. Melancholies strive for perfection and worry excessively about potential harm and their privacy. They prioritize security over taking risks and avoid indulging in any form of risk. They worry about various aspects of their lives, including their relationships, jobs, and even the fear of sinning against nature. Their temperament also plays a role in triggering fear.

3. **Fear of Failure:** The fear of failure can hold you back from achieving your goals. Aliko Dangote, a successful businessman, encountered skepticism when he decided to build a refinery in Nigeria. Despite the doubts from colleagues and friends, he took the risk and believed that not trying would already be a failure.

Thomas Edison also faced countless failures before inventing the light bulb. It took him 1000 attempts before he succeeded. Similarly, Harland Sanders the CEO of Kentucky Fried Chicken (KFC) didn't achieve success until he was over 65 years old, after recording several failures.

Often, your negative mindset can contribute to your perceived failures. Whether it's in marriage or academics, it's essential to change your mindset and eliminate thoughts of failure and limitations. With determination and a willingness to overcome self-doubt, you will achieve greatness.

4. **Fear as a Result of Limitations:** Here's a quote that says, "Let your fear be your indication of growth." Limitations are a state of mind; human beings have the capacity to do anything. Even God knows this; that's why He came down Himself to stop man from their plans in the Book of

Genesis 11:1-8 (KJV) And the whole earth was of one language, and of one speech.

And it came to pass, as they journeyed from the east, that they found a plain in the land of Shinar; and they dwelt there.

And they said one to another, Go to, let us make brick, and burn them thoroughly. And they had brick for stone, and slime had they for morter.

And they said, Go to, let us build us a city and a tower, whose top may reach unto heaven; and let us make us a name, lest we be scattered abroad upon the face of the whole earth. And the LORD came down to see the city and the tower, which the children of men builded. And the LORD said, Behold, the people is one, and they have all one language; and this they begin to do: and now nothing will be restrained from them, which they have imagined to do. Go to, let us go down, and there confound their language, that they may not understand one another's speech. So the LORD scattered them abroad from thence upon the face of all the earth: and they left off to build the city.

Myles Munroe, of blessed memory, once said that the richest place in the world is...

If I may ask you, where is the richest place in the world?

Just answer within yourself before we continue.

Myles Munroe said the richest place in the world is not the World Bank, not the White House, but the CEMETERY. Yes, are you shocked? Don't be. The reason is, millions of people have tread this part of the world with thousands of potentials within them but were unable to tap into these potentials and actualize them until they died. They were all buried with those potentials. Just imagine if Thomas Edison thought the way you're thinking and limited himself or got discouraged; there wouldn't be light today, and if there were, it wouldn't be in his name.

Have you heard about Nicholas James Vujicic (born 4 December 1982)? He is an Australian-American Christian evangelist and motivational speaker of Serbian descent. He has tetra-Amelia syndrome, a disorder characterized by the absence of arms and legs. Despite this, he grew beyond his limitations and affected his world positively.

Consider this: until tomorrow, students will be studying Aristotle, Auguste Comte, and Emile Durkheim; the world will not forget Bill Gates, Elon Musk, Papa Ayo Babalola, John Wesley, Myles Munroe, and Apostle Paul, etc., because they made an impact in their world and didn't allow fear to limit them, even Jesus Christ our king was once like you, but will be celebrated till tomorrow.

My advice to you, my dear friend reading this is, don't allow fear to limit you from achieving your goals. I say this to you, as long as your plans are legal and won't violate societal norms, go for it. With Christ Jesus, you're strengthened. How do you overcome your fear? Below are some working and proven tips that have worked for millions of people.

HOW TO OVERCOME FEAR:
Overcoming fear can be achieved through several effective tips.

1.   **Pursue Knowledge:** Whenever fear arises, it may stem from a lack of understanding and knowledge. To combat this, prioritize self-education. The more you read, the brighter and smarter you become. Self-education is invaluable.

2.   **Learn from Experts:** Study individuals who have excelled in your desired path. Pay close attention to their lives and principles, and apply them to your journey for success.

3.   **Choose Your Circle Wisely:** The people you surround yourself with will greatly impact your life. Surround yourself with those who uplift and inspire you. Avoid being a lion among sheep; instead, discover yourself and align with like-minded peers.

4.   **Seek God's Guidance:** Remember, you are first a spirit before being a physical being. Seek the guidance of God through Christ Jesus. Discover His will for your life and align your thoughts with His. *(Jeremiah 29:11-13 (KJV) For I know the thoughts that I think* *toward you, saith the **LORD**, thoughts of peace, and not of evil, to give you an expected end. Then shall ye call upon me, and ye shall go and pray unto me, and I will hearken unto you. And ye shall seek me, and find me, when ye shall search for me with all your heart.*

5. **Embrace the Holy Spirit**: Overcome limitations and fears by being filled with the Holy Spirit. The Holy Spirit grants the grace to fill you with love and faith. For further insights into the ministry of the Holy Spirit and how to be filled with Him, I encourage you to explore my book titled **THE LIGHT**.

THE DESIRE TO BE IMPORTANT
"The deepest urge in human nature is 'the desire to be important." — Dr. John Dewey.

According to this quote, your desire to be important shapes your true character. In simple terms, what makes you feel important defines the most significant aspects of your life. When these aspects are threatened or taken away, it can lead to shame, depression, and even suicidal thoughts.

Kindly consider what makes you feel important, your relationships, family, children, job, faith, fame, titles, material possessions like a car, and so on. If you share what gives you a sense of importance, it will reveal your character.

According to my research, the desire to be important is a significant cause of depression. Many people become depressed when what makes them feel important is taken away. Take, for example, a woman who has been in a relationship for over four years, anticipating marriage. Both families have met, and the wedding has been announced. Just days before the wedding, she receives the devastating news that her fiancé has called it off. What becomes of her?

1. The wedding announcement had gone viral.

2. She faces intense shame from everyone around her, including her family.

3. She grapples with thoughts like, "Where will I start from?"

Another example is a man with a well-paying job, who is respected for being able to provide for his family's needs. Suddenly, he loses his job. What becomes of him?

Have you asked yourself why losing something insignificant, like a small amount of money, doesn't bother you as much as losing something precious, like a loved one, children, or valuable material possessions such as gold or diamonds worth millions? This is because the things that make us feel important are deeply tied to our sense of self and well-being."

This brings us to another important point: What makes you feel important?

Kindly consider this question carefully. The factors that make people feel important vary from person to person. Our interactions can significantly impact others' mental health, often pushing them toward depression or worse due to how we relate to them. Let me explain.

Our daily interactions be it between parents and children, bosses and subordinates, landlords and tenants, or pastors and congregants play a crucial role in shaping mental health. Each individual has a sense of importance, which may stem from their achievements, family, relationships, career, and accumulated wealth. In these contexts, feelings of importance and personal ego come into play, affecting everyone, young and old alike.

Let's consider the parent-child relationship. Children can be both wonderful and curious. Suppose a child is inquisitive, frequently asking questions. Ideally, parents should encourage and guide them. However, if instead, the child is condemned and subjected to derogatory remarks, their confidence diminishes. Over time, the child may lose the courage to ask questions, either at home or in school. Many children today suffer from serious mental health issues because the adults around them undermine their self-worth with hurtful words.

Boss and Subordinate Relationship

Have you ever witnessed a scenario where intelligent, wealthy, and capable adults burst into tears because they were insulted by their boss or colleague?

If yes, you understand the gravity of the situation. If not, that's fine; we're all learning. As a boss, if you undermine and tarnish your workers' mental health, you leave them with fear instead of respect and self-worth.

Many people today feel mentally detached from their jobs, even though they physically continue. Why? Because they no longer see value in themselves due to their boss's constant derogatory statements. Going to work feels like entering a lion's den. This principle also applies to pastor-member relationships. Dear leaders, correct your members with love and appreciate them, even when they are wrong. Remember how Jesus treated Peter and how God forgave David. Judge with love and not with the sword.

Furthermore, husbands, when was the last time you appreciated your wife with kind words? And wives, do the same for your husbands. Dear boss, remember, your authority is tied to that office chair. The day you retire, that authority ends. Even if you own the business, you will eventually say goodbye to that office. Always remember, "You will be remembered for both the problems you solved and the ones you caused." Strive to be a source of happiness rather than a pillar of sorrow.

Finally, the best way to respect an individual's sense of importance is by loving them and giving them a listening ear. This aligns with the true nature of Jesus, our greatest mentor in leadership and human relations. The best way to solve problems is by listening without judgment and being rational. Always put yourself in the shoes of the person you're dealing with before you nail them. Remember, good and godly attitudes enhance our world.

PART 2

SCIENTIFIC AND SOCIAL TREATMENT OF DEPRESSION
(DEPRESSION GOLDEN TREATMENT APPROACH)

CHAPTER 5

GOLDEN APPROACH TO DEPRESSION

1. Mindfulness and Meditation:

Mindfulness practices involve paying attention to the present moment without judgment, which can help individuals cultivate awareness and reduce stress. Meditation techniques, such as deep breathing exercises, body scans, and mindful walking, can promote relaxation and emotional well-being. For example, practicing mindfulness while savoring a cup of Nigerian tea or observing the natural beauty of Nigeria's landscapes can enhance sensory awareness and foster inner peace.

2. Cognitive-Behavioral Therapy (CBT):

CBT is a widely used therapeutic approach that focuses on identifying and challenging negative thought patterns and behaviors associated with depression. By learning to reframe distorted thinking, individuals can develop healthier coping strategies and improve their overall mood. For example, recognizing and challenging negative self-talk, such as "I'm not good enough," with more balanced and realistic thoughts such as I can do it, I'm not mediocre, can help individuals regain a sense of control and self-esteem as I share in the previous chapter on limiting oneself and measure to overcome it.

3. **Social Support:**

Building a strong support network of family, friends, or support groups can provide valuable emotional support and encouragement. Sharing experiences, expressing emotions, and receiving validation from others can reduce feelings of isolation and foster a sense of connection and belonging. For example, participating in community gatherings joining a local support group, and becoming a worker in church can provide opportunities for socialization and mutual support.

4. **Physical Activity:**

Regular exercise has been proven to be an effective mood booster and stress reliever. Engaging in physical activity releases endorphins, neurotransmitters that promote feelings of happiness and well-being. For example, dancing in church, playing music, swimming, taking a walk, and dancing away your sorrow, there was this friend of mine, while going through a difficult challenge instead of her to be depressed she chose to dance away her sorrow all she does is play music from her phone and dance or engaging in outdoor activities like hiking or cycling can provide both physical and mental health benefits.

5. **Creative Expression:**

Engaging in creative activities such as painting, writing, music, or crafting can provide an outlet for self-expression and emotional release. Creative expression allows individuals to channel their thoughts and feelings into a tangible form, fostering a sense of empowerment. For example, attending a workshop can provide opportunities for self-discovery and connection with others, aside from this, we have thousands of videos on YouTube which can add value to you.

6. **Self-Care Practices:**

Prioritizing self-care is crucial for nurturing our physical, emotional, and mental health. By participating in activities that foster relaxation, pleasure, and personal development, you can replenish your energy and restore balance to your life. For instance, taking yourself on a solo outing whether it's a meal, a movie, or a leisurely stroll, doesn't require a companion; it's an opportunity to invest in your own happiness. Regardless of your circumstances, take advantage of the resources available to you to cultivate a fulfilling existence that is, Create your world with your wealth. Even in countries where access to amenities may be limited, such as Nigeria where electricity can be unreliable, equip your home with solar power and enjoy a comfortable lifestyle.

7. **Setting Boundaries:**

Establishing clear boundaries and limits in relationships (defining relationships) and activities can help individuals protect their mental and emotional health. Saying no to excessive demands or obligations and prioritizing self-care and personal needs can prevent burnout and reduce stress. For example, setting boundaries around work hours or social commitments and carving out time for relaxation, distancing yourself from relationships that cause you headaches, can promote balance and well-being.

8. **Seeking Professional Help:**

When coping strategies alone are not sufficient, it's important to seek help from qualified mental health professionals. Therapists, counselors, psychiatrists, and other healthcare providers can offer guidance, support, and evidence-based treatments tailored to individual needs. For example, attending therapy sessions with a culturally competent therapist who understands Nigerian cultural norms and values can facilitate healing and growth.

By incorporating these strategies and techniques into your daily life, you can develop a personalized toolkit for coping with depression and overcoming obstacles on the journey to saying goodbye to it. Remember, progress may be gradual, and setbacks are a natural part of the process. With perseverance, support, and determination, it is possible to reclaim joy, vitality, and hope in life.

OTHER TIPS INCLUDE:

1. Stay in Touch: Maintain connections with friends, family, or support groups. Social interaction can provide comfort and support during difficult times find someone you can confide in and open up with disturbing thoughts.

2. **Be More Active**: Incorporate physical activity into your routine, even if it's just a short walk. Exercise releases endorphins, which can improve mood and energy levels.

3. **Face Your Fear:** Confronting fears and anxieties can diminish their power over you. Start small and gradually work your way up to bigger challenges. Furthermore, fear will always keep you from what will yield value and bring you to greater heights. I remember when I started writing, my greatest fear was who would purchase my book, but was motivated by a friend who happened to put it on her WhatsApp status that "Start the rubbish gradually you will improve". The rubbish I started yesterday was what you're reading today. "Start with something", "start from somewhere."

4. **Try Eating a Healthy Diet:** Include more fruits and vegetables in your meals.

Nutrient-rich foods can positively impact mood and overall well-being.

5. **Have a Routine**: Establishing a daily routine can add structure to your life and give you a sense of purpose. Make time for activities you enjoy and prioritize self-care.

6. **Seeking Help for Depression:** Don't hesitate to reach out to a therapist, counselor, or mental health professional. They can provide valuable support, guidance, and treatment options. Do away with what will people say. People don't matter but your life and well-being are what matters.

7. **Stay Engaged:** Keep yourself occupied with hobbies, projects, or volunteer work. Staying busy can distract you from negative thoughts and provide a sense of accomplishment. What saved one of my friends from depression was the ability for his parents to discover this tip, by taking him along to their workplace and getting him involved in something that would prevent his mind from negative thoughts.

CHAPTER 6

UNDERSTANDING LOVE LANGUAGES: A KEY TO PREVENTING DEPRESSION

In the journey to bid farewell to depression, one of the most powerful tools we have at our disposal is understanding the concept of love languages. Developed by Dr. Gary Chapman, love languages are how individuals give and receive love. They include words of affirmation, acts of service, quality time, physical touch, and receiving gifts. By recognizing and appreciating these languages, we can foster deeper connections with our loved ones and build strong emotional support networks, ultimately helping to prevent depression.

Step 1:

1. **Words of Affirmation:** For some, hearing words of encouragement and praise is essential for their emotional well-being. By expressing appreciation and affirmation to those whose love language is words of affirmation, you can boost their self-esteem and provide validation for your partner or friend, helping to counter negative thoughts and feelings associated with depression. Below are examples of Words of Affirmation: Words of Affirmation:

- "You mean the world to me."

- "I appreciate all the little things you do for me."

- "You're so talented and capable."

- "I love how caring and compassionate you are."

- "Your smile brightens up my day."

2. **Acts of Service:** Study that friend, partner, or colleague in your place of work whose love language is acts of service, and try this because actions often speak louder than words. Offering practical help and support, such as assisting with chores or running errands, can alleviate stress and lighten the load for them. This will impart a sense of feeling that they are not alone in their struggles, which will serve as a powerful antidote to feelings of hopelessness. Practical examples of Acts of Service are:

- Cooking a meal for your partner after a long day.

- Doing household chores without being asked.

- Taking care of errands or tasks on behalf of your partner, friend, or colleagues.
- Offering to help with work or projects they're struggling with.

- Giving them a massage or helping them relax after a stressful day.

3. **Quality Time:** Spending meaningful, uninterrupted time together with your spouse, friends, and colleagues is crucial for individuals whose love language is quality time. By engaging in activities, they enjoy and actively listening to their thoughts and feelings, we demonstrate our care and strengthen our connection with them. This sense of companionship and understanding can serve as a protective measure against the isolating effects of depression. Below are workable examples:

- Going for a walk together and having meaningful conversations.

- Planning a weekend getaway just for the two of you.

- Have a regular date night where you spend focused time together.

- Turning off all distractions and spending an evening just enjoying each other's company.

- Doing activities together that you both enjoy, whether it's cooking, hiking, or playing games.

4.   Physical Touch: Human touch has a profound impact on our emotional well-being, particularly for those whose love language is physical touch. Hugs, cuddles, and other forms of affectionate touch can release oxytocin, the "love hormone," reducing stress and promoting feelings of security and belonging. Incorporating physical touch into our interactions can help combat feelings of loneliness and disconnection, which are key risk factors for depression.

Examples include:

- Holding hands while walking or sitting together.

- Hugging and cuddling on the couch while watching a movie. (For married couples)
- Giving massages or back rubs to help them relax.

- Kissing them goodbye or hello each day. (For married couples)

- Sitting close to each other and making physical contact during conversations.

5.   Receiving Gifts: While material possessions may seem superficial, for individuals whose love language is receiving gifts, thoughtful gestures can carry deep emotional significance. These gifts serve as tangible symbols of love and appreciation, reminding recipients that they are valued and cherished. Such gestures of generosity can provide comfort and joy, countering the negative emotions often associated with depression.

Examples include:

- Surprising them with their favorite flowers, chocolates, phones, cars, etc.

- Buying a meaningful gift that shows you've been paying attention to their interests.
- Making something by hand, like a scrapbook or a piece of art.

- Giving them something they've been wanting for a while, even if it's small.

To uncover your friends' or partner's love language, pay close attention to their expressions of affection and the areas where they might express dissatisfaction. Listen for cues like "Can't you greet?" or "When was the last time you kissed me?" "When was the last time you got me a gift?" "When last did you help me in the kitchen?" These seemingly minor complaints often reveal where they desire more love and attention. By addressing these concerns, you can better understand and communicate in their preferred love language. Remember, within your grievances lies your love language.

By understanding and speaking the love languages of our partners, friends, and loved ones, we can create a supportive environment that fosters emotional well-being and resilience. Building strong, meaningful connections based on mutual understanding and appreciation acts as a powerful deterrent against depression. As we embrace the language of love, we pave the way for brighter days ahead, bidding farewell to depression one heartfelt expression at a time.

STEP 2:

POSTING THE PICTURE OF YOUR LOVED ONES WITH LOVELY CAPTIONS AS A KEY TO THE PREVENTION OF DEPRESSION:

Posting pictures of your loved ones, friends, and spouse on social media with a lovely caption is another working tip that has contributed to preventing depression in several ways:

1. **Fostering Connection:** Sharing photos of your loved ones on social media helps maintain a sense of connection, especially in today's digital age where physical distance and individualistic mentality often separates friends and family. Seeing images of loved ones can evoke feelings of warmth, closeness, and belonging, reducing feelings of loneliness and isolation that can contribute to depression.

2. **Creating Positive Memories:** Posting pictures of happy moments spent with loved ones, such as birthday parties, graduation ceremonies, and last visits, often creates a digital album of positive memories. Revisiting these memories through photos can evoke feelings of joy, gratitude, and contentment, lifting moods and countering negative emotions associated with depression.

3. **Building Social Support:** Sharing pictures of your loved ones such as that of your lovely wife, children, and Colleagues allows your social network to see and engage with the important people in your life. Friends and family members may comment on or react to these posts, expressing admiration, support, and love. This virtual support network can provide emotional validation, encouragement, and reassurance, strengthening mental resilience and reducing the risk of depression.

4. **Encouraging Expression of Affection:** Posting pictures of your loved ones on social media provides an opportunity to publicly express affection and appreciation for them. When last did you celebrate your angel with magic words, are not aware this act of recognition and celebration can reinforce the bonds of love and friendship between both of you? Not only that, it will also enhance feelings of connectedness and belongingness, which are protective factors against depression.

5. **Promoting Gratitude:** Sharing images of your loved ones encourages you to focus on the positive aspects of your relationships and experiences, thereby reducing the lack of trust and arguments that may arise between both of you. Reflecting on meaningful moments that you've shared can help strengthen your bond and reduce the likelihood of developing depressive symptoms.

6. **Spreading Joy:** Your posts depicting moments of love, happiness, and togetherness can serve as a source of inspiration and joy for others in your social network. By sharing positivity and uplifting content, you contribute to a supportive online community that fosters emotional well-being and happiness

Consider posting his or her picture today and see the profound impact it could have.

You might just be saving a life.

PART 3

FAITH PERSPECTIVE ON DEPRESSION

CHAPTER 7

DEPRESSION AND BELIEVERS

In the journey from darkness to light, believers are taught that the Lord has overcome the world. However, some followers wonder why they experience depression or depressive disorder despite being born again and working in the light. It is important to remember that the Lord never promised a life without tribulations, but instead foretold that we would face challenges. Moreover, believers must understand the distinction between temptation and tribulation. Temptation arises from our own sinful desires, providing an opportunity for Satan to operate in our lives. On the other hand, tribulation is a test or exam regarding our stand in faith ordained by God to elevate us to a higher level in our faith. It may involve challenging circumstances that ultimately bring glory to God or serve as a testimony to others.

Moreover, it's essential for believers to discern between temptation and tribulation. Temptation arises from personal desires or sinful inclinations, providing an opening for Satan to exert influence. Conversely, tribulation serves as a test or trial, allowing believers to ascend to higher spiritual levels. It's a time when God permits challenging circumstances to glorify Himself or convey a message to the world. For instance, Christ's sacrifice exemplifies how trials can lead to greater spiritual revelation and redemption."

Understanding the dynamics of temptation and tribulation is crucial. Temptation, stemming from sin, necessitates seeking mercy from God. Conversely, when facing tribulation, grace becomes our vital resource for overcoming. Job's resilience stemmed from the Lord's grace, as did Jesus Christ's endurance through the crucifixion, fortified by prayer and divine strength. As believers, embracing prayer and discernment enables us to navigate unavoidable trials. Failure to grasp these distinctions often leads to despair.

Let's delve into the roots of depression among believers:

1. Depression As A Result Of Striving For Lordship

Upon accepting Jesus, believers commit to two agreements:

i.   Submitting to Jesus as their Lord entails seeking His approval before any action, akin to a servant-master relationship.

ii.   Acknowledging Jesus as Saviour involves exchanging one's old life for His, a transaction for redemption.

Many believers selectively adhere to the terms of their faith, prioritizing control and rationality over spiritual awareness. This tendency leads them to focus on worldly matters, neglecting the guidance of the spirit. In response, God, as a loving father, intervenes to reclaim His followers who have strayed.

Often, individuals unwittingly replace their devotion to God with reliance on various earthly influences such as authority figures, relationships, or material success. This misplaced allegiance can lead to spiritual disconnect and, ultimately, estrangement from God. Rather than questioning or resisting God's intervention, believers should humbly acknowledge His mercy and guidance.

The distinction between surrendering to God's lordship and straying from it is subtle but crucial. To illustrate, some believers prioritize familial or financial support over God, attributing their blessings solely to their sources (from your work, your boss, and your parents) rather than acknowledging God's role. This misattribution can lead to arrogance and a false sense of self-sufficiency.

Moreover, some individuals, whether consciously or not, assume a godlike status in the lives of others they stand as godfathers, receiving adoration and dependence that rightfully belongs to God alone. Biblical examples, such as Nebuchadnezzar and Herod, underscore the dangers of such arrogance and the importance of maintaining reverence for God.

Nebuchadnezzar, the king of Babylon, ruled over a powerful kingdom. Despite his thriving lordship, he arrogantly claimed glory meant for God. In response, God humbled him by causing him to suffer from mental depression for seven years (Daniel 4:28-33). Despite Nebuchadnezzar's faults, God showed him mercy and love when he eventually humbled his mind; hence his kingdom was restored unto him.

Daniel 4:34-37 (KJV) And at the end of the days I Nebuchadnezzar lifted up mine eyes unto heaven, and mine understanding returned unto me, and I blessed the most High, and I praised and honoured him that liveth forever, whose dominion is an everlasting dominion, and his kingdom is from generation to generation: And all the inhabitants of the earth are reputed as nothing: and he doeth according to his will in the army of heaven, and among the inhabitants of the earth: and none can stay his hand, or say unto him, What doest thou? At the same time my reason returned unto me; and for the glory of my kingdom, mine honour and brightness returned unto me; and my counsellors and my lords sought unto me; and I was established in my kingdom, and excellent majesty was added unto me. Now I Nebuchadnezzar praise and extol and honour the King of heaven, all whose works are truth, and his ways judgment: and those that walk-in pride he is able to abase.

Similarly, Herod's pride led him to demand worship as if he were a deity, leading the people to hail him as God. Many pastors, bosses, and even average believers in church are in these categories. This provoked God, and he was struck down by the angel of the Lord.

Acts 12:21-23 (KJV) And upon a set day Herod, arrayed in royal apparel, sat upon his throne, and made an oration unto them. And the people gave a shout, saying, It is the voice of a god, and not of a man. And immediately the angel of the Lord smote him, because he gave not God the glory: and he was eaten of worms, and gave up the ghost.

Allow me to illustrate this biblical lesson with a practical example. There was a devout Christian who enjoyed a close relationship with God. However, upon securing a lucrative job, his focus shifted from God to his wealthy employer. Despite the boss's favor and financial support, the man's devotion waned as he began idolizing his boss. This continued for years until new employees, influenced by Satan, turned against him, leading to his dismissal.

After being sacked, the man returned to God in tears and fasting, questioning why such misfortune had befallen him. Through prayer, God revealed to him that, the man had chosen his boss over Him, leading to his downfall. However, in His mercy, God allowed these trials to teach man a valuable lesson. Once he repented and realigned his priorities, God elevated him once again.

This story serves as a reminder that idolizing anything above God, whether it be a job, a relationship, or material possessions, can lead to spiritual downfall. Just as the man in this story learned, recognizing and rectifying these misplaced priorities will lead to restoration and blessings from God.

2. **Depression As A Result Of Lack of Understanding of Process and Timing:**

Ecclesiastes 3:1-4 (KJV) To everything there is a season, and a time to every purpose under the heaven;

A time to be born, and a time to die; a time to plant, and a time to pluck up that which is planted;

A time to kill, and a time to heal; a time to break down, and a time to build up;

A time to weep, and a time to laugh; a time to mourn, and a time to dance;

Many believers demonstrate their love for God and align with His will, yet they often overlook the importance of studying God's dimensions, as revealed through the experiences of our biblical forefathers (Abraham, Joseph, and David). According to the general Apostle Joshua Selma, the Bible encapsulates three fundamental aspects:

- The principles of God

- The prophecies of God

- The promises of God

These three elements shape the life of every believer. When God imparts His promise to an individual, akin to the encounters of our faith ancestors such as Abraham, Joseph, and David, there ensues a sense of excitement prompting us to share this divine revelation with friends or relatives. While this enthusiasm is natural, it is imperative to note that the fulfillment of such prophecies may not be immediate, leading some to doubt its authenticity. However, as scripture emphasizes, God's word remains steadfast.

The question arises: why do certain prophecies fail to materialize? Drawing from insights gleaned from the teachings of esteemed spiritual leaders and scripture, it becomes evident that every significant promise or prophecy from the Lord announces a journey of preparation. This journey entails diverse forms of instruction and refinement, essential for navigating the path toward fulfillment. Joseph exemplifies this principle; his journey, marked by tribulations, served as a crucible for acquiring profound understanding and endurance, ultimately positioning him for divine purposes. Notably, Joseph's initial vision doesn't come with the journey to prison, or meeting himself in Potiphar's house; rather, all these afflictions were to facilitate his growth through his learning process.

From the moment a prophecy is received until its fulfillment, there exists a transitional period filled with invaluable lessons and revelations. Those who bypass this preparatory phase often falter upon attaining fulfillment, lacking the requisite understanding to endure. A clear example of this is King Saul and King David. For years, King David was running from one cave to another despite being anointed as king around the age of 12-15 years old, he never walked into this reality till he was 30 years of age. However, King Saul was given a prophecy, and with no time became king of Israel without serious guidance and teaching from the Lord.

Recognize that the challenges you're encountering don't signify abandonment by God, but rather an opportunity for personal growth. Embrace the guidance of the Holy Spirit and absorb the lessons intended for by him. Instead of resisting, align yourself with the flow.

Reflect on the story of the coconut tree and the orange tree, amidst the wind, the coconut tree will bend and never struggle with the wind, because it understands the transient nature of the storm knowing it's just for a while, thus safeguarding its fruits. Conversely, the orange tree, in its resistance, will never bend rather it struggled with the wind and lost its precious fruits.

Stop struggling with your present challenges; instead, cooperate with the Holy Spirit to help you overcome them. Remember to call on Jesus; He's with you in the boat, just as the apostles did.

I can perceive someone asking, "What of I that was raped by my father?"

Humm well, it's an incredibly distressing situation, and it evokes deep sympathy. I'm truly sorry you've had to endure such a harrowing experience. Amidst all, here is the word of God

Jer.29.11 For I know the plans I have for you," says the LORD. "They are plans for good and not for disaster, to give you a future and a hope. (NLT)

But amidst the pain, there's an opportunity for growth. Have you imagined any insights from your situation? Imagine encountering someone sharing a similar story with you, his or her heart, heavy with sorrow. Your firsthand understanding in regards to your experience would enable you to empathize profoundly and offer genuine solace or solution to his or her problem; in addition, the lord has a better plan for you.

I heard you say Busayo you know I was a devoted Christian before this happened to me!

Fine, despite you being a devoted Christian prior to the incident, it may occur to you that why is God silent in the face of my suffering? But know this: God did not condone such evil; it was the handiwork of Satan's deceit. No this, as a believer even in our trials, we find strength. You survived because the Lord fortified you, shaping you for such adversity.

Consider this: Had Joseph been David or David been Joseph, the outcome of their story might have been different. You're persevered because God knows your capacity and future. As you read this, breathing and alive, recognize that your survival is a testament to your purpose.

James.1.2 Dear brothers and sisters, whenever trouble comes your way, let it be an opportunity for joy. (NLT)

Joyce Meyer, too, emerged from a similar background, refusing to let her past define her future. Today is the day to reclaim your destiny. I understand the depths of depression, having battled it myself, alongside loved ones. By releasing the past and letting it go and entrusting your future to the hands of the Holy Spirit, which will help replace hopelessness with faith and joy.

Are you wondering if there's hope for you after having multiple abortions?

Or you've slept with different men, to the point of losing count?

Absolutely. Jesus is a merciful God who forgives. Take, for instance, Shola Allyson—yes, the same Sola Allyson who had several abortions before Christ found her and was forgiven by God. Today, she's happily married with children. Your situation isn't unique, and there's provision for you if you return to your Father.

And if you're thinking, 'Busayo, I'm involved in cyber fraud, clubbing, and promiscuity, is there any hope for me?' Christ is your hope. He has already forgiven you even before you committed those sins. All you need to do is acknowledge Him as your savior, surrender your life to Him as your Lord, turn away from your old ways, and let his mercy speak in your life.

1 Chronicles 16:34 (KJV) O give thanks unto the LORD; for he is good; for his mercy endureth for ever.

Dear friend reading this book consider yourself lucky that you're alive to tell your story, remember many never had a second chance, but here you are. All you have to do is to submit totally, not mentally but totally to Jesus as your lord and Saviour, so has to have a new beginning. Having you've done that. Permit me to tell you, it's time to gather your strength, heal from your past, and join the fight against child abuse, depression, and the kingdom of darkness, by using your story to motivate others and winning SOUL for Jesus Christ. I see a mighty warrior within you, ready to conquer the world. Together, let's make a stand and bring light to those in darkness.

Lastly, understanding God's process and timing is paramount for believers. Through perseverance, faith, and a willingness to learn, one can navigate life's challenges and fulfill their divine destiny.

3.   Depression As A Result Of Teaching on Trusting God

I intentionally break this down to clarify how God prepares his children, separating it from process and timing. Before the world witnesses your manifestation as a son of God, you must dwell, walk, and build quality relationships with God as his child. After passing several tests, you graduate to sonship, manifesting the glory of your Father. Even when faced with challenges, as a son, you know where to turn. Despite the possibility of punishment, you still have the courage to apologize and seek forgiveness from your Father.

Consider the story of the prodigal son, who, after squandering his father's property, chose to face the consequences and return to his father, rather than seeking comfort elsewhere. Note that God's judgment differs from man's; He values humility and submission. He may grant forgiveness or even bless you abundantly, but that is at His discretion.

Another biblical example is the contrast between David and Saul. Saul relied solely on the power of prophets, while David spent 15-17 years learning to trust God for the fulfillment of His promises. Saul's dependence on prophets led him to seek forgiveness through Samuel, whereas David, having walked with God, sought forgiveness through fasting, prayer, and supplication.

Your current circumstances are not meant to destroy you but to draw you closer to God, to understand His ways, and to rely on Him when facing challenges while manifesting His glory.

Depression stemming from prophetic-related issues is a serious concern. Prophecies delivered in the name of 'thus saith the Lord' have shattered countless homes, families, and lives. While receiving divine messages is a privilege, it can also be perilous to build one's entire life around them. Remember, you are not only a child of God but also a cherished creation, endowed with divine promises. Just as a loving father shields his children from harm, God desires your happiness and well-being.

Numerous prophecies, such as:

"Thus, saith the Lord you will die soon."

"Thus, saith the Lord you will never amount to anything."

"Thus, saith the Lord you will never conceive again."

"Thus, saith the Lord you will never find a good job."

"Thus, saith the Lord you will never marry a good person."

May sound true and accurate. However, as the recipient of such words, it is crucial to reconsider:

Am I in good standing with God?

Is my salvation secure?

Am I obedient to God's will?

If not, there are legitimate reasons for these prophecies to manifest. Yet, if you are in alignment with God, understand that you possess the authority to alter your destiny. Step into your priestly office and boldly declare your desires before your Heavenly Father. Many believers overlook the authority bestowed upon them through Christ Jesus. Every believer has direct access to God Almighty and the throne of grace.

To those who are yet to surrender their lives to Him, remember, that you are still children of God according to this scripture:

Psalms 82:6 (KJV) I have said, Ye are gods; and all of you are children of the most High.

Regardless of any prophetic words spoken against you, the Lord has a plan in place. When a product malfunctions, the best course of action is to return it to where it was purchased, as there is typically a warranty for replacement or repair. Similarly, your Heavenly Father offers amendments to your life; He can remodel or repair it. You need not worry; all He asks is for you to turn to Him, confess your sins, and pray for forgiveness, rather than seeking guidance from 'LOCAL TECHNICIANS' such as pastors and prophets, who can only convey what they perceive. You possess the power to rewrite the negative script of your life Jesus is as close to you as you can ever imagine.

Biblical example

Let the story of King Hezekiah inspire you. Prophet Isaiah, renowned for his accurate prophecies and for prophesying the coming of Jesus Christ, was sent to King Hezekiah

Isaiah 38:1-5 (KJV) In those days was Hezekiah sick unto death. And Isaiah the prophet the son of Amoz came unto him, and said unto him, thus saith the LORD, Set thine house in order: for thou shalt die, and not live. Then Hezekiah turned his face

*toward the wall, and prayed unto the **LORD**, and said, Remember now, **O LORD**, I beseech thee, how I have walked before thee in truth and with a perfect heart, and have done that which is good in thy sight. And Hezekiah wept sore. Then came the word of the **LORD** to Isaiah, saying, Go, and say to Hezekiah, thus saith the **LORD**, the God of David thy father, I have heard thy prayer, I have seen thy tears: behold, I will add unto thy days fifteen years.*

Despite the prophecy delivered, King Hezekiah did not confront or argue with Isaiah. Instead, he turned to God Almighty, his creator, and fervently prayed until God answered his plea.

My Personal Experience

A few years ago, I found myself battling depression due to multiple prophecies I received from various sources. These prophecies all foretold a grim fate for me, I was told I would die, never will I achieve anything in life, and will never complete my university education. This onslaught of negativity left me heartbroken and directionless, spiraling into a state of depression. Despite my struggles, I felt as though no one around me truly understood the turmoil I was experiencing.

In a moment I remembered the story of King Hezekiah, and I turned to God, seeking solace and guidance. Through fervent prayer, tears, supplication, and fasting, I pleaded for mercy, and the Lord graciously answered my prayers. It was through a friend, whom I believe God sent to me Julius Ibukun, that I found salvation in Jesus Christ. Since then, my life has undergone a radical transformation where once there was hopelessness, now there is hope; where once there was darkness, now there is light.

Today, I stand as a living testimony to the power of God's grace, done with university education and still alive. Just as the renowned musician Shola Allyson overcame her own battle with depression, she refused to let her past dictate her future. Instead, she chose to turn her experiences into a message of hope for others.

Shola's story, shared at mass 4.0, inspired me to entrust my cares to Jesus Christ, likewise, I'm sharing mine with you today.

1 Peter 5:7 (KJV) Casting all your care upon him; for he careth for you.

Now, I urge you, dear friend, to heed this message: do not allow negative prophecies or words to drag you into darkness. Jesus desires for you to walk in the light, reflecting His glory for all to see. Your life has the potential to be a powerful testament to His love and grace. Embrace this truth, and let Jesus illuminate your path to a brighter future.

4. Depression As A Result Of Demonic Possession

The concept of demonic possession is primarily rooted in religious and spiritual beliefs. Individuals experiencing depression or depressive disorder may attribute their condition to demonic possession or influence.

There are distinct differences between the two phenomena:

Demonic possession occurs when the devil inhabits or dwells within an individual. This is often associated with people who do not believe in Jesus and are not filled with the Holy Spirit, as it is believed that two spirits of different lords cannot inhabit the same body.

Demonic influence, on the other hand, can affect spirit-filled Christians who believe in Jesus as their Saviour. Although demons cannot inhabit them, they can linger around them, oppress them, influence their decisions, and manipulate their thoughts, making it seem as though they are the originators of those thoughts.

To gain a better understanding of this topic, let's examine a biblical example from the book of Mark 5:1-20 and Luke 8:26-39:

Jesus Christ arrived in a region called Gadara, where the inhabitants were unfamiliar with the message of salvation or the gospel of Jesus, indicating a community of sinners.

According to Luke 8:27, upon disembarking from the ship, Jesus encountered a man who was naked, homeless, and living among tombs a manifestation of severe mental disorder.

According to the Bible, it was recorded that he had been possessed by demons for a long time, which simply means he had been mentally ill for a prolonged period. The book of Mark 5:2-3

Mark.5.2-3 Just as Jesus was climbing from the boat, a man possessed by an evil spirit ran out from a cemetery to meet him. This man lived among the tombs and could not be restrained, even with a chain. (NLT)

Clarifies that the demon in this man was so strong that no one could bind him, no physician could diagnose him, and not even chains could restrain him, as he broke everything, as mentioned in verse 4.

Mark 5:4-5 (KJV) Because that he had been often bound with fetters and chains, and the chains had been plucked asunder by him, and the fetters broken in pieces: neither could any man tame him. And always, night and day, he was in the mountains, and in the tombs, crying, and cutting himself with stones.

In verse 5 of the book of Mark, it was recorded that this man would always be on the mountain or in the tombs, crying, just like you reading this, crying or feeling sad without any specific reason or as a result of what had happened to you. Aside from crying, he would also cut himself, just as used a razor blade, knife, and other dangerous objects. Besides, the inner voice may urge you to hurt yourself, jump from upstairs, isolate yourself from everyone, detest even your loved ones, and at times, indulge in evil things, which lead to tears and self-condemnation bringing past experiences to mind and urging you to commit acts of violence. These thoughts are not your own but are possessed or influenced by the devil within or around you.

For those who are believers and filled with the Holy Spirit, yet still feel depressed, the issue may be that you are being influenced by the devil. However, the power within you is stronger than him; he cannot possess you but can frustrate your life due to a lack of knowledge and revelation in the word of God guiding your dominion.

Mark 5:6-7 (KJV) But when he saw Jesus afar off, he ran and worshipped him, And cried with a loud voice, and said, What have I to do with thee, Jesus, thou Son of the most high God? I adjure thee by God, that thou torment me not.

Continuing, the man with the mental disorder did something very special and surprising when he saw Jesus. Let's see what he did in verse 6. When he saw Jesus, he ran and worshipped him. Immediately, the demons in him reacted with a loud voice and begged Jesus not to cast them out, as power had met with power, and the lesser power had to bow. However, Jesus did not yield to them, as the devil cannot decide for Jesus what to do.

Mark 5:9-13 (KJV) And he asked him, what is thy name? And he answered, saying, My name is Legion: for we are many. And he besought him much that he would not send them away out of the country. Now there was there nigh unto the mountains a great herd of swine feeding. And all the devils besought him, saying; Send us into the swine, that we may enter into them. And forthwith Jesus gave them leave. And the unclean spirits went out, and entered into the swine: and the herd ran violently down a steep place into the sea, (they were about two thousand ;) and were choked in the sea.

Thus, Jesus cast out the demons, as mentioned in verses 9-13 because he has to save his child. It's important to note that it was not the man negotiating with Jesus, as the devil had taken hold of him and possessed his mind, controlling his entire life. The man had no say in what was happening to him. Jesus cast out the demons, including the one called Legion.

Mark.5.15 When they came to Jesus, they saw the man who had been possessed by the legion of demons, sitting there, dressed and in his right mind; and they were afraid. (NIV)

Fast-forward to verse 15 of the same chapter, the man was completely free and came back to his right mind, which means he's fully restored to his senses. Many who are currently depressed have lost a part of their minds to the devil. Therefore, you need to regain your mind and your true self. If you're reading this and have been experiencing demonic oppression or influence, I urge you to follow the example of that man by running to the feet of Jesus.

Yes, to the feet of Jesus. You may ask, 'How?' It's very simple. All you need to do is surrender your life to Jesus as your Lord and Saviour.

Once you do that, there's a transfer of lordship, and the power of the Lord will come upon you. This marks the beginning of your journey to reclaim your mind. Surrendering to Jesus makes it easy to break free from the power of darkness that manipulates your mind.

If you're ready, kindly join me in prayer.

Pray Out Loud

Dear Jesus, I confess that you are my Lord and Saviour. I believe in my heart that you're the son of God, you came to this world and died for me and God raised you from the dead. By faith in Your Word, I receive my salvation now in Jesus's name. Thank you, Lord Jesus, for saving me

Amen!

Congratulations!

There's more to what you've just done. I encourage you to visit any Bible-believing Church near you and ask to speak with the pastor. Explain that you've just given your life to Jesus through reading a book. They will guide you on what to do next. Alternatively, you can message me through any of my contact information for a free copy of my book, THE LIGHT. I'll forward the e-copy to you to serve as a guide in developing your relationship with Jesus and the Holy Spirit.

Thank you and God bless you. Once again, congratulations for taking this bold step.

5. Depression As A Result Of Desiring To Hear The Audible Voice Of God

Desiring to hear the audible voice of God, many believers have found themselves oppressed by demonic influences. While there's nothing wrong with longing to hear God's voice or the spirit of the Holy Ghost, the issue often lies in the pursuit without proper discernment and knowledge.

Hosea.4.6a my people are destroyed from lack of knowledge.

"Because you have rejected knowledge, I also reject you as my priests; (NIV)

As a Christian and a child of God, it's not a sin to desire to hear from God or the Holy Spirit, but the error often occurs in lacking discernment. It's true that God does speak audibly to His children, but such occurrences are rare and usually happen on special occasions.

For instance, we recall the moment when Jesus spoke to Paul loudly from heaven on his way to Damascus, (Act 9:1-7) a voice that even those around him heard.

Acts.9.7 The men with Saul stood speechless with surprise, for they heard the sound of someone's voice, but they saw no one! (NLT)

However, it's essential to understand that God communicates with His children in diverse ways, always in accordance with Scripture.

Having the Scripture as a guide helps us discern whether the voice we hear is from the Lord or from a familiar spirit. If what we hear contradicts Scripture or doesn't glorify God, then it's not from Him. As children, we don't dictate how our Heavenly Father communicates with us; instead, He knows the best way to speak to each of us.

Regarding the Holy Spirit, the more we fellowship with Him, the more He reveals to us how He communicates with His people.

Romans 8:14 (KJV) for as many as are led by the Spirit of God; they are the sons of God.

One of the reasons why people may experience depression or mental illness is their pursuit of hearing the audible voice of God or seeking the voice of the Holy
Spirit, which can sometimes lead to hearing demonic voices. I've witnessed scenarios where individuals, in their quest for divine communication, end up encountering familiar spirits due to their lack of discernment. Many find themselves in this situation, sincerely desiring to hear from God but forgetting that His voice is often heard through the inner ear of the spirit, not the physical ear. Just as we have spiritual eyes, we also have spiritual ears. Note this scripture as well.

To clarify this topic, I'll draw an example from the writings of Kenneth E. Hagin, a renowned preacher and author. From his popular book (How You Can Be Led By The Spirit Of God).

I preached at a meeting in Oregon in the summer of 1954. At the close of one of the first services, I was laying hands on the people who stood in the long prayer line. I asked each one what they had come forward for before I ministered to them. When I came to one woman, her husband who had her by the arm said, "We have come for my wife's healing." He told me she'd had a mental breakdown. I did not know this woman was a former Sunday school teacher in that church, nor that her husband was a deacon in the church. But when I laid my hands on her, in a second of time just like it ran off on a television screen, I knew all about this situation. I knew it by the spiritual gift called the word of knowledge (1 Cor. 12:8). I saw this woman in a large tent meeting in one of Oregon's largest cities. I saw her sitting in the congregation with thousands of people. She heard the evangelist tell how God spoke to him in an audible voice and called him into the ministry. I do not doubt that. This woman failed to realize, however, that this evangelist did not ask God to speak to him that way. God just did it on His own. We have no right to seek that God would speak to us in an audible voice. If God told us He would in His Word, then all of us would have a right to claim it. But this evangelist hadn't even particularly expected God to speak in that way—but if God wants to, He can, and He saw fit to do so in that particular case.

At the time this woman heard the evangelist tell that, she was all right mentally. But then she began to seek God to speak to her in an audible voice—and the devil accommodated her. She began to hear voices. They drove her insane. She was now about to be taken to the asylum for the second time.
I also saw this in the spirit: Her husband had taken her to this same evangelist for deliverance. She did not receive deliverance. Now her husband blamed that evangelist. Then her husband had taken her to another leading evangelist. She had failed to be delivered. Now her husband was angry with that other evangelist too. I knew she would not be delivered if I laid hands on her, and then he would be angry with me. So I took my hand off of her. I said to the man, "Take your wife into the pastor's study. Wait there. When I finish this line, I will talk with you."

After we were finished with the healing line, the pastor and I went into the study together.
"First of all," I said to this couple, "I have never been to Oregon before. I have never seen you folks before. I don't even know if the pastor knows you. "The pastor said, "He's one of our deacons."

"Well," I said, "the pastor will tell you he has not told me anything. "Then I related what I had seen. The deacon said, "That's exactly right."

"Now," I said, "I will tell you why I didn't minister to your wife. You see, she wants to hear these voices. "Then I said, "She is not so far gone mentally that she doesn't know what I am saying. "She spoke up, "I know exactly what you are saying. "I said, "Sister, you are not going to be delivered until you want to be delivered. As long as you like it the way it is—as long as you want to hear these voices—you are going to hear them. "She said, "I want to hear them." As long as a sinner wants to live in sin, God will let him live in sin. But if he wants to change, God will meet him and deliver him. And even though a person is a Christian, that does not mean he loses his free moral agency. He does not become a robot—a machine whereby God pushes a button and he automatically has to do whatever God desires. He is still a free moral agent. As long as he wants things like they are, they will stay that way. But if he wants to cooperate with God, he can be helped. This woman said, That's the way I want it." I said, "I knew that the minute I touched you. That's the reason I didn't minister to you. As long as you want it this way, it's going to be this way.

Simply intending to hear a voice won't bring healing; it requires your active cooperation. Instead of seeking voices, focus on cultivating a relationship with God. Study His Word, pray, and meditate on what you've learned. Allow the Holy Spirit to minister to you directly and lead you. Scripture tells us, **For as many as Are Led By The Spirit Of God, they are the sons of God**,' not 'For as many as **Seek The Audible Voice Of God**.' May you receive grace and wisdom to align your actions with Scripture. Always remember any voice that contradicts Scripture, fails to glorify God, or lacks peace should be disregarded.

6.   Depression Arising from a Test of Faith

Job 1:6-8 (KJV) Now there was a day when the sons of God came to present themselves before the LORD, and Satan came also among them. And the LORD said unto Satan, whence comest thou? Then Satan answered the LORD, and said, from going to and fro in the earth, and from walking up and down in it. **And the LORD said unto Satan, Hast thou considered my servant Job, that there is none like him in the earth, a perfect and an upright man, one**

that feareth God, and escheweth evil?

The highest form of attestation any human can receive from God is His affirmation of their faith. Yet, despite this divine attestation to Job, why do trials and depression afflict honest and faithful individuals like Job?

The word "depression" is derived from the Latin word "deprimere," meaning "to press down." As believers, we often encounter life's challenges that press us down more than we can imagine. Sometimes, these are the very things we fear, as narrated by Job in the scriptures (Job 3:25). We do everything possible to prevent these fears from becoming reality.

Job 3:25 (KJV) For the thing which I greatly feared is come upon me, and that which I was afraid of is come unto me.

Being depressed may not necessarily stem from your sins or the path you are treading. Instead, it can arise because God has given Satan the legal ground to test you, just as He did with Job.

Take note: Job was without sin and took every precaution to avoid sinning against God. When his children gathered and feasted, he sacrificed unto God according to their numbers (Job 1:2-5).

Job 1:2-5 (KJV) And there were born unto him seven sons and three daughters.

His substance also was seven thousand sheep, and three thousand camels, and five hundred yoke of oxen, and five hundred she asses, and a very great household; so that this man was the greatest of all the men of the east. And his sons went and feasted in their houses, everyone his day; and sent and called for their three sisters to eat and to drink with them. And it was so, when the days of their feasting were gone about, that Job sent and sanctified them, and rose up early in the morning, and offered burnt offerings according to the number of them all: for Job said, It may be that my sons have sinned, and cursed God in their hearts. Thus, did Job continually.

Similarly, you may not have any besetting or secret sins, yet you might face various challenges. Remember, it might be just a test of your faith in God.

Many believers today face various challenges for which they have no specific explanation. The tragic part of these experiences is the mockery they often endure from fellow believers, who may view those going through difficulties as sinners, much like Job's wife and friends did.

One thing I've learned about God and His dealings with man is not to be too quick to judge anyone. Instead, I strive to be empathetic to their situation. I either ask the Holy Spirit if I should step in to provide a solution (if I have one) or join them in prayer. Remember, every person is acting according to the book and script written for them, and we all carry our crosses separately.

For you reading this book, let's learn not to be quick to judge anyone facing tests or trials of any kind. Additionally, some might not go through such tests because of God's mercy. Therefore, I advise standing in the gap and seeking God's mercy, regardless of our attainments in Jesus Christ.

To you, dear friend, whose challenge is profound, I advise seeking God's mercy. No matter how faithful and holy we strive to be, we are like filthy rags before God. (Isaiah 64:6)

Philippians 3:9 (KJV) And be found in him, not having mine own righteousness, which is of the law, but that which is through the faith of Christ, the righteousness which is of God by faith:

Our righteousness is not obtained by our power or works but is a free gift from God. I pray the Lord gives you the grace to endure your trials and emerge victoriously in Jesus' name. Healing is available through Jesus Christ. Hallelujah.

CHAPTER 8

RELATIONSHIP AND HEARTBREAKS

The impact of heartbreak has wrought more harm than good upon both believers and unbelievers alike. Many individuals, both men and women, are grappling with depression or depressive disorders as a result of being heartbroken by their partners—individuals they may have been willing to sacrifice everything for. I won't pass judgment for finding yourself in relationships that lead to heartbreak, but I sincerely sympathize with you.

Some have managed to overcome and share their stories, while others have tragically succumbed to the darkness. It's not because they didn't want to survive, but rather because they were ensnared by their demons before encountering or allowing the light of Jesus to penetrate their minds. As for you reading this, I congratulate you for being one of the very few who lived to tell the testimony.

It's important to acknowledge that depression often feels like an evil force that consumes the mind, akin to a garment of heaviness wrapped around you from the pit of hell. No matter how powerful or strong your spirit may be, battling depression often requires the grace of God to rescue you from its grip.

During the period of depression, you hear a series of negative voices like:

- "It's all over!"

- "Where will you find the strength to begin anew?"

- "You'll never find someone good again."

- "You prayed, yet God failed you."

- "God is unfaithful."

- "End your life."

- "This world is cruel; you don't have to endure its cruelty."

- "Everyone despises and hates you."

These voices stem from the pit of hell as a result of the garment of heaviness the devil wraps around you, obscuring any illusion of hope or positivity in your life and surroundings.

What you may not realize is, that the moment you become aware of your situation and begin to pray, especially in the Holy Ghost (speaking in tongues), you tap into inner strength, edify your spirit, and are endowed with the presence of God. This causes the demon to flee, as it cannot withstand such power. The scripture says

1 Peter 5:8-10 (KJV) Be sober, be vigilant; because your adversary the devil, as a roaring lion, walketh about, seeking whom he may devour: Whom resist stedfast in the faith, knowing that the same afflictions are accomplished in your brethren that are in the world. But the God of all grace, who hath called us unto his eternal glory by Christ Jesus, after that ye have suffered a while, make you perfect, stablish, strengthen, settle you.

Permit me to share the story of a beautiful young lady who was once a victim of depression

In this story, we encounter a beautiful lady whose engagement crashed despite all preparations being in place for the awaited day. Just before the anticipated event, the guy delivered a devastating blow, ending their relationship abruptly. He swiftly moved on with another woman, leaving her shattered.

Overwhelmed by despair, she collapsed and found herself in the hospital. Upon her discharge, she sought refuge with her pastor, grappling with severe depression.

Despite her efforts to move on, the wounds in her heart remained unhealed. She was clothed with the garment of heaviness from the pit of hell; she made three attempts to end her life. The final one stands out vividly...

On that fateful day, just as she used to experience, she was tormented by relentless thoughts from the pit of hell, she found herself in a private environment. Unable to resist the overpowering darkness, she grasped a knife, which she took from home as she rapped it with her rapper to prevent anyone from seeing it. Yet, just as she was about to succumb to the darkness, a divine intervention unfolded. In a moment of clarity. An open vision materialized before her eyes. The Holy Spirit brought forth the image of the man who had shattered her heart, compelling her to reconsider her actions. In this vision, she witnessed two dark spirits attempting to pull him away, as they pulled him away, he was yarning and trying to beckon her to withhold the knife (the Lord Jesus is faithful because this was the only picture in her mind, as such the Lord has to use the picture to speak to her), and he pleaded with her to stop her impending self-destruction.

As the vision was playing, divine scripture echoed within her weakened spirit, and she struggled to find the strength to confess those scriptures. With the assistance of the Holy Ghost, she mustered the courage to utter a confession, invoking the power of God's word to break the hold of the demons that had beclouded her mind. With great calmness, she withdrew the knife.

At that moment, she experienced a profound sense of peace. It was then she shared with me the song that had sprung forth from her spirit:

'I'm the one you've shown me mercy, you've shown me mercy.

Afterward, she began speaking in tongues, gaining more strength and capacity with each utterance.

However, it's crucial to recognize that the voices you hear, or thoughts within you aren't your own; they belong to agents of darkness from hell, which Jesus referred to as liars.

John 8:44 (KJV) Ye are of your father the devil, and the lusts of your father ye will do. He was a murderer from the beginning, and abode not in the truth, because there is no truth in him. When he speaketh a lie, he speaketh of his own: for he is a liar, and the father of it.

To anyone contemplating ending his or her life, your situation may not unfold like hers did. You might not be granted a second chance (The act of being rescued from your suicide attempt). To prevent a story that touches the heart, I implore you to run to the feet of Jesus; He has everything you need to survive.

No matter how long your relationship which led to heartbreak or your marriage that ended in a crash, Jesus offers a replacement. The story of water turned into wine serves as an example of your circumstances. Jesus can bring meaning back into your life if you allow Him. Give Him your heart; let Him in, and He will surely fill you with joy once more.

For my dear brothers and sisters in the Lord, your experience (failed relationship) may be as the reward of his great love for you, because he will never allow his children astray. Why not turn back to your first lover? Reignite the fire, and allow Him to glorify Himself in your life.

Remember, the Holy Ghost provides a garment of praise to replace the heaviness Satan has clothed you.

PART 4

DEPRESSION DIAMOND TREATMENT APPROACH

CHAPTER 9

DIAMOND APPROACH

Introducing the Diamond Approach: A Faith-Based Way to Beat Depression: When you're struggling with depression, finding comfort and strength in faith can make a big difference. The Diamond Approach explained in this book, relies on faith to help you heal and bounce back. This method comes from personal experience, born out of dealing with depression firsthand.

Depression often makes it hard to see any hope, leaving you feeling lost and hopeless. But the Diamond Approach offers a ray of hope, showing you a way forward by believing in something bigger than yourself. It's all about having faith and using it as a solid base to rebuild your life.

In this Chapter, we'll look at the ideas and actions behind the Diamond Approach, exploring how it can help you cope with depression and come out stronger in the end. Come along with me on this journey of faith and resilience as we uncover the bright spots hiding in the darkness of hopelessness.

1. **The Journey of Faith.**

Our Lord Jesus Christ has provided for every soul burdened by the weight of depression. His promise, as stated in the book of Is*aiah 61:3 (KJV) To appoint unto them that mourn in Zion, to give unto*

them beauty for ashes, the oil of joy for mourning, THE GARMENT OF PRAISE FOR THE SPIRIT OF HEAVINESS; that they might be called trees of righteousness, the planting of the LORD, that he might be glorified. Is a guaranteed for you to believe that Jesus is interested in your mental health and ready to lift you from hopelessness, and depression into comfort and a better life?

- **How to access this promise:**

Firstly, surrender your life to Jesus as your Lord and Savior. Jesus, the Light of the World, is present to dispel every darkness that Satan has cast upon you. His death has secured divine light and eternal life for you, liberating you from every demonic influence, whether born of imagination or from the realm of darkness.

Here are examples of demons often born of our own imaginations:

- SELF-DOUBT

- SELF-JUDGEMENT

- FEELING UNWORTHY and INSIGNIFICANT

- FEELING SERIOUS

- BAD HABITS

- UNCERTAINTY

- FEELING POWERLESS

Yet, beyond these, there are real demons from the pit of hell that cause depression. As the Bible teaches us in ***Ephesians 6:12 (KJV) For we wrestle not against flesh and blood, but against principalities, against powers, against the rulers of the darkness of this world, against spiritual wickedness in high places.***

With this understanding, victory lies in having Jesus Christ. Those who have Christ fight from a position of victory, as He has already won their battles. How do you claim this victory? Simply put, by invoking the name of Jesus, as *Philippians 2:9-11 (KJV) Wherefore God also hath highly exalted him, and given him a name which is above every name: That at the name of Jesus every knee should bow, of things in heaven, and things in earth, and things under the earth; And that every tongue should confess that Jesus Christ is Lord, to the glory of God the Father.*

This tongue includes everything that doesn't glorify the name of God such as depression, and addiction of any kind. Command them into the obedience of God through Jesus Christ.

I urge you to engage in this fight with wisdom, leveraging the power of Jesus' name as your greatest weapon to overcome all the powers of darkness.

- **Be filled with the Holy Ghost, not with wine :(Holy Spirit and Holy Ghost mean the same thing)**

One of the essential aspects of being filled with the Holy Ghost is to deliver us from every weariness of heart and spirit of heaviness, which may drive one to seek solace in alcoholic drinks. If you're tired of dwelling on those burdensome thoughts, remember this wisdom in *Proverbs 31:6-7 (KJV) Give strong drink unto him that is ready to PERISH, and wine unto those that be of HEAVY HEARTS. Let him drink, and forget his poverty, and remember his misery no more.*

This verse speaks to the temporary relief sought in alcohol for those facing burdensome circumstances. However, true and lasting comfort comes from being filled with the Holy GHOST, who offers peace and solace beyond any earthly substance. That's why he's referred to as the COMFORTER

John 14:16 (KJV) And I will pray the Father, and he shall give you another

Comforter, that he may abide with you forever;

However, In Ephesians 5:18, the Bible encourages believers to be filled with the Holy Ghost, who brings comfort, guidance, and peace. Rather than turning to substances like wine for the comfort of pain or to cope with depression, relying on the Holy Ghost will provide true solace and strength.

The question is, do I need the Holy Ghost after giving my life to Jesus?

The answer is No, receiving the Holy Ghost isn't compulsory but mandatory, mandatory in the sense that, eternal life is God's gift to every man (through Jesus Christ) but the gift of the Holy Ghost is for God's children hence as a child of God I perceived rejecting your father's gift is pride. The core value of the Holy Ghost in believers' lives is for spiritual growth and empowerment, any believer who is wise to attain maturity and exercise his full potential here on earth must long for the gift. The Holy Spirit is a gift from God specifically for His children, who have accepted Jesus Christ as their Lord and Saviour and believed in His ministry to exercise His fullness here on earth.

Why Do I Need The Holy Spirit?

1. To empower us to become children of God. (John 1:12-13)

2. The Holy Spirit imparts the life of God within us. (Romans 8:11)

3. The Holy Spirit leads us into a deeper love for God, as He is the very essence of God's love. (Romans 5:5)

4. The Holy Spirit reveals Jesus Christ as a living and active presence in our lives, not merely a historical figure. (John 14:26)

5. The Holy Spirit equips us with the power of God to live victorious lives and the ability to witness to nations. (Act 1:8)

6. The Holy Spirit fosters intimacy and fellowship with God. (2 Corinthians 13:14)

7. The Holy Spirit teaches us about God's ways and righteousness. (John 16:13)

8. The Holy Spirit helps us transcend our fleshly desires, enabling us to exhibit godly character and bear spiritual fruit, leading to personal transformation and growth. (Galatians 5:22-23).

- **How To Be Filed With Holy Ghost**

1. The key to unlocking anything in the kingdom is faith. Without faith, nothing operates effectively. Once you firmly believe that the gift is from God and meant for you, and you will receive it with unwavering faith, that's all that's required. The additional tips are merely supplemental and provide basic guidance for receiving the gift.

2. The evidence of being baptized in the Holy Spirit is speaking in tongues; According to Scripture, when Paul encountered twelve believers in Ephesus, he asked them if they had received the Holy Ghost since they believed. They replied that they hadn't even heard of the Holy Ghost. Paul then inquired about their baptism, and upon learning they were baptized with John's baptism (water baptism), he explained the significance of baptism in the Holy Ghost through Jesus Christ. After Paul laid his hands on them, they received the Holy Ghost, spoke in tongues, and prophesied (Acts 19:2-7 KJV). Speaking in tongues allows believers to communicate mysteries to God directly (1 Corinthians 14:2 KJV). When speaking in tongues, believers are speaking directly to God Almighty.

Notice

During the baptism of the Holy Ghost, some individuals experience the fire of God and think they will be cut off just like the prophets. No. It's important to note that this experience does not cut you off from your surroundings; you remain aware of your environment. Speaking in tongues isn't automatic, because individuals have a role to play in cooperating with the Holy Spirit. The words spoken may not be familiar, as the Spirit wills, and the action originates from within, as described in **John 7:38 (KJV) He that believeth on me, as the scripture hath said, out of his belly shall flow rivers of living water.**

Speaking in tongues allows believers to communicate mysteries to God directly (1 Corinthians 1 **Corinthians 14:2 (KJV) For he that speaketh in an unknown tongue speaketh not unto men, but unto God: for no man understandeth him; howbeit in the spirit he speaketh mysteries.**

 When speaking in tongues, believers are speaking directly to God Almighty and the essence of speaking in tongues is for your edification (to charge yourself).

3. Magnifying God: It's important to note that evil spirits will never magnify God; instead, they flee from His presence because true believers carry the fire of His holy Spirit. According to Scripture (Acts 10:15, 45-46 KJV), those who have received the baptism of the Holy Spirit magnify God. When Peter witnessed the Gentiles receiving the gift of the Holy Spirit and speaking in tongues, he was astonished. As you prepare your heart to receive, may you also magnify God in Jesus' name. Receive the Holy Spirit with open arms.

Remember, as God's child, your loving heavenly Father desires to equip you with the supernatural power you need to live victoriously. Just as Lu*ke 11:10, 13 assures, everyone who asks receives, everyone who seeks finds, and to everyone who knocks, the door will be opened. Your heavenly Father eagerly gives the Holy Spirit to those who ask Him.* All you have to do is ask, believe, and receive!

Pray Out Loud

Thank you, Father, for this priceless gift of Yours. I believe You have already given it to me for this purpose. Father, I acknowledge my need for Your power to live this new life. Please fill me with Your Holy Ghost. I believe I have received it right now! Thank You very much for baptizing me. Holy Ghost, You are welcome in my life.

Congratulations!

You are now filled with God's power, the Holy Spirit. Words from an unknown language will rise from your stomach (belly) to your mouth (See 1 Corinthians 14:14). Pay close attention and speak up. By speaking out loud in faith, you are releasing God's power from within and strengthening yourself in the Spirit.

It makes no difference whether or not you felt anything when you prayed for the Holy Ghost. If you believe in your heart that you have received it, God's Word promises you that *'whatsoever ye desire, when ye pray, believe that ye receive them, and ye shall have them' (Mark 11:24, KJV).* God always keeps His promises, so believe Him!

Congratulations once again!

2.   Unseal the Book (Reading of the Bible):

The Bible, often referred to as the "Word of God," contains messages of hope, healing, and encouragement. Regularly reading and studying the Bible allows individuals to gain insights into God's love, purpose, and promises, which can help alleviate feelings of despair and hopelessness.

Based on my experience in my walk with Christ, I often advise my friends to begin their Bible reading journey with the New Testament. This recommendation stems from witnessing individuals who have misunderstood or misinterpreted the Old Testament, leading to confusion or error. Starting with the New Testament provides a solid foundation in understanding the teachings of Jesus and the principles of Christianity. Once familiar with the New Testament, one can then delve into the Old Testament with greater clarity and context.

Remember, the entire New Testament serves as an explanation and fulfillment of the Old Testament. Before delving into the Scriptures, it's essential to pray for guidance and illumination from the Holy Spirit. May you receive His grace and light as you unseal the book In Jesus' name, amen.

3.   Embrace the Spirit of Praise

Praising God, even in the midst of difficulties, can shift our focus from problems to the greatness of God. As *Psalm 34:1 declares, 'I will bless the Lord at all times; his praise shall continually be in my mouth.'* Engaging in praise and worship uplifts the spirit, bringing a sense of joy and peace that transcends circumstances. This truth has been tested and affirmed by many, including Bishop Oyedepo, Pastor E. A Adeboye. I implore you to receive the garment of praise given to you by Christ Jesus.

4. **Make Prayer a Lifestyle**

Prayer is essential communication with God, and the Bible encourages believers to pray without ceasing (1 **Thessalonians 5:17).** Through prayer, we can cast our anxieties and burdens upon God, finding comfort and strength in His presence. Developing a habit of prayer fosters a deep connection with God and assures us of His care. As *Matthew 7:7 reminds us, 'Ask and it will be given to you; seek and you will find; knock and the door will be opened to yo*u. 'In addition, remember the Elijah how he prayed down heavens.

James 5:17 (KJV) Elias was a man subject to like passions as we are, and he prayed earnestly that it might not rain: and it rained not on the earth by the space of three years and six months.

I charge you to pray into your happiness, your destiny and your freedom.

"We become through prayer"

5. **Develop the Habit of Fellowshipping with Other Believers**

Hebrews 10:25 urges believers not to forsake gathering together but to encourage one another. Fellowship with other believers provides opportunities for support, encouragement, and the impartation of grace that one may not experience when alone. Together, we strengthen and uplift each other in our faith journey.

I. **The maximizing the power of confession;**

Confessing the word of God, or scripture, is a potent tool for overcoming depression. Here's why:

II. **Renewing the Mind:** Speaking and meditating on scripture renews the mind. Depression often stems from negative thought patterns and distorted perceptions. Confessing God's promises reshapes our thinking, replacing despair with hope and pessimism with faith.

Rom.12.2 Do not be conformed to this world (this age), [fashioned after and adapted to its external, superficial customs], but be transformed (changed) by the [entire] renewal of your mind [by its new ideals and its new attitude], so that you may prove [for yourselves] what is the good and acceptable and perfect will of God, even the thing which is good and acceptable and perfect [in His sight for you]. (AMP)

Let's read from another version

Rom.12.2 Don't copy the behavior and customs of this world, but let God transform you into a new person by changing the way you think. Then you will know what God wants you to do, and you will know how good and pleasing and perfect his will really is. (NLT) ii. **Source of Strength:** Scripture is a source of strength during difficult times. When we confess passages about God's love, faithfulness, and promises, we tap into a reservoir of divine strength that uplifts and sustains us. ***Phil.4.13 For I can do everything with the help of Christ who gives me the strength I need. (NLT)***

III.   **Combating Lies with Truth**: Depression often feeds on lies—about ourselves, our circumstances, and our worth. Confessing scripture exposes these lies and replaces them with the truth of God's Word. For example, declaring "Psalms 139:14 (KJV) **I will praise thee; for I am fearfully and wonderfully made:** marvelous are thy works; and that my soul knoweth right well.

IV.   **Inviting God's Presence:** When we confess scripture, we invite God's presence into our lives. His Word is alive and active **Hebrews 4:12 (KJV) For the word of God is quick, and powerful, and sharper than any two-edged sword, piercing even to the dividing asunder of soul and spirit, and of the joints and marrow, and is a discerner of the thoughts and intents of the heart.** Bringing comfort, peace, and assurance. As we speak His promises, we experience His nearness and find solace in His love.

V. **Empowering Declarations:** Confessing scripture is an act of faith and declaration. By speaking God's Word over our lives, we assert our trust in His faithfulness and authority. This empowers us to rise above depression's grip and walk in victory. *John.8.36 So if the Son liberates you [makes you free men], then you are really and unquestionably free. (AMP)*

Confessing the word of God is a transformative practice that renews the mind, strengthens the spirit, combat lies with truth, invites God's presence, and empowers us to overcome depression. It's not merely reciting words; it's an intentional, faith-filled declaration of God's promises and truth over our lives.

By adopting this approach and following the outlined above, you embark on a journey towards guaranteeing your happiness, freeing yourself from depression, and stabilizing your mental health. By embracing the spirit of praise, making prayer a lifestyle, and developing the habit of fellowshipping with other believers, you open doors to inner peace, strength, and resilience. These practices not only nurture a deeper connection with God but also foster a supportive community that uplifts and encourages. May this path lead you to a life filled with joy, peace, and spiritual fulfillment. Remember Jesus is interested in your mental health.

CHAPTER 10

REAL LIFE STORY TO MOTIVATION YOU

Before I release you finally, I will share with you the story of a 34-year-old lady whose past was about scattering her marriage, and how she overcame by combining the two, the golden approach and the diamond approach in solving her problem.

Media. (Smile)

**Here is a story of Mirabel, as
narrated by herself. Written
by Tife Oni www.zikoko.com
Last Updated April 19, 2023**

I had a rough childhood. I grew up in Mushin, Lagos state, Nigeria. in the early 90s and was raised by a single mother. Up until she died in 2020, my mother claimed my father was dead, and I decided to act according to my mother's tale.

I was my mother's only child and was mostly alone after school when she had to hustle for us to survive. My mum took on as many odd jobs as possible — from cleaning and washing to selling food at canteens. During the weekends, I'd join her to work wherever she was working that week.

When I finished secondary school in 2006, I knew we couldn't afford university, so I put my efforts into hustling. I got my first job as a salesgirl in an electronic store when I was 17. Not long after, I entered a rebellious phase. Most nights, I didn't go home to the one-room apartment I shared with my mother, choosing to stay with friends instead. She didn't bother too much about me. It was Mushin (Lagos); everyone was pretty wild. Now, I wish she did. Around this time, I met my baby daddy, Kunle. He owned an electronic store in the same market. And I started dating him, moving in with him almost immediately without my mother's knowledge.

Three months into our relationship, I was pregnant. Now my mother needed to know. He went with his brother to tell my mother he wanted to marry me. My mother couldn't do anything because I was already independent and was now pregnant. There was no "marriage". I just kept living with him till I had my son.
And that's when the trouble started. I couldn't work anymore because I had to take care of my son, so Kunle took care of all our expenses. But he soon got frustrated
 I'm not sure why and started acting out and beating me at night. Due to my husband's abuse, I decided to return to my mother's house.

By my son's first birthday, my relationship with my mum was getting strained. I was open to other possibilities. So, I listened to Kunle when he came back to beg me to return home with him. I figured he'd had enough time to change.
Besides, I badly needed to leave my mum's place.

I moved back in with Kunle in 2008 and was pregnant again within six months. When I was close to delivery, Kunle suggested I move back in with my mum to have my child so I'd have someone to take care of me, promising to send money regularly. I listened to him and went back to my mother.

Do you know this man sent money only once and then disappeared? He must have planned it for some time — I went to look for him at his shop some weeks after I had my second son and was told he'd packed out. I haven't seen him since that time. There I was, a single mother of two at 20 years old. I wanted to die. For weeks, I was in shock. I thought my life was over. My mum noticed **I WAS BATTLING DEPRESSION** and surprisingly stepped up. She encouraged me to focus on doing something with my life. She didn't want me to continue the cycle she was in.

With her watching the kids, I enrolled in a polytechnic in 2010. It was one of the most difficult things I'd ever done. I'd shuttle between school and use any available time to do anything I could to make money. I started doing hair and selling cheap data to support my fees and send money home to my mother since I mostly lived in school. God must've decided to show me mercy because one of my fellow students, also a hair client, carried my matter on her head. She didn't know about my struggles or my kids — no one knew — but she noticed I was always hustling and would disturb me to follow her to the school fellowship.

Trust you're following?

Let's see what happened next after an invitation to school fellowship.

I eventually did one day in my second year, and my life changed. **I gave my life to Christ** and became fairly active in the fellowship. They had something called "indigent support", which was financial support for struggling students, and I got the allowance with the help of my client-turned-friend. It was a lifeline and helped pay part of my tuition for the rest of the time I was in school. I also met the man I'd marry, George, at the fellowship. He was a senior friend of the fellowship he graduated years before and only came to worship with us occasionally. I don't know what he saw in me, but we became close friends in my final year. He even followed me to my mum's house once. There, he met my kids but just assumed they were my siblings. It didn't help that my kids weren't used to me I was hardly around They knew I was their mum, but they called me Mimi, as my mother did, and called my mother, mummy. I didn't see a reason to explain to George because I didn't think it was important. **Frankly, I just didn't want to be judged.**

George was so good to me. So, when he eventually told me of his feelings after I graduated in 2015, I was too scared to tell him the truth. I thought he'd run the other way, and I didn't want to lose the only good thing that'd happened to me in a long time. I told my mother, and she also suggested keeping it to myself, since the children wouldn't live with me. We got married that same year but didn't have children immediately. George wasn't worried about it, and never pressured me. But three years in, I started getting worried and made him visit the doctor with me.

Maybe I shouldn't have. One of the first questions the doctor asked us was if I'd ever been pregnant. **I froze.**

George didn't notice and immediately answered no, but my conscience kept pricking me. It felt like God was telling me it was time to tell my husband the truth. I struggled with it for about a week before I mustered the courage to do it. ***I spoke to our pastor and his wife and told them*** about it. Then they called him to set up a meeting at our house. My husband thought they wanted to pray for us. As soon as they arrived on the day we set; I went on my knees before my husband. He was extremely confused, but our pastor explained what I'd told him. I'd never seen my husband so disappointed. I was expecting anger, but nothing could have prepared me for the heartbreak I saw in his eyes. **He didn't utter a word for about an hour.**

Then he told me to stand up and that he'd forgiven me. I was shocked. Our pastor prayed for us and left.

It wasn't over, though. He didn't talk to me or say anything about the revelation for weeks after that meeting. We greeted each other, ate together, and slept on the same bed, but the tension was so thick I couldn't touch him. I begged and begged, but he said he needed time to process it. I could literally see my marriage falling apart.

After she noticed what had befalling her, let's see how she overcame it.

SO, I FASTED AND PRAYED LIKE NEVER BEFORE

One day, I knelt to beg him again, and this one did it. I eventually broke through to him. It was a long healing process, but I'm thankful we overcame it. He made sure we became closer with my sons and even insisted they move in with us when my mother died two years later in 2020. I'm still learning how to be a mother to them I was practically absent for more than a decade of their lives but George treats them like his own. I don't know why I ever thought he wouldn't accept them. He's become closer to them than I might ever be, which warms my heart daily.

I hope you enjoyed the story. Better still, this story comes with different meanings and teachings. Mirabel's fear of being judged ended her in what would have taken her happiness. If not for God's mercies and intervention.

In regards to the story, you could see How she adopted what a called those approaches in resolving her ordeal.

Learn how to seek God for forgiveness as the scripture says in the book of 2 **Chronicles 7:14 (KJV) If my people, which are called by my name, shall humble themselves, and pray, and seek my face, and turn from their wicked ways; then will I hear from heaven, and will forgive their sin, and will heal their land.**

If God can forgive you, man will also do. Go now and amend your life.

CONCLUSION

In conclusion, the key to your healing lies within these four pillar rules which are: Education, Belief, Effort, and Discipline. These rules formed the foundation of an unbreakable, unbelievable, and unshakable life. By living according to these rules and applying the lessons learned in this book, there is nothing you cannot create, nothing you cannot achieve, and no dream too big, no challenge too large. No person or group can hinder you, and there are no limits to what you can accomplish with the golden and diamond approaches if strictly followed.

Reading this book has opened you up to revelation and exposed you to realities around you. However, it doesn't end there; you must believe in what you've learned. Belief prepares you to experience the truths shared in this book. The difference between you and those who have not encountered this book lies in your belief. Embracing these approaches and tips will lead to the benefits outlined in this book, propelling your healing and wholeness.

Reading without belief is merely a wasted effort. Your faith is essential to your healing. Once you believe, your efforts and actions become the next crucial steps toward accessing your healing.

The effort, or the spirit of never giving up, is vital. Merely reading and believing in what you've read isn't enough; you must take action and implement the tips accordingly. Taking action will allow you to create the difference you're hoping for. Like myself years ago, the actions I took saved me from depression. Take action now and become an overcomer. While the results may not be immediate, rest assured they are on their way.

Lastly, discipline is the key to maintaining the manifestation of the power that has healed you. Be disciplined in applying all the principles and approaches learned in this book. Do not claim healing and then neglect what you must continually do. Remember, Satan is relentless; your healing is a continuous process. The more you allow the light to shine in your mind, embrace the ministry of the Holy Spirit, and remain intentional about your walk with Him, the stronger you become. With the Holy Ghost, your healing is secured. Love you and eagerly await to see you radiating His glory. One Love.

ABOUT THE AUTHOR

Olamiti Busayo Imoleayo is a Believer and a student of medical sociology in the Department of Sociology, Adekunle Ajasin University. He's very passionate about believer's and unbelievers' mental well-being. The passion to help individuals navigate the path of loneliness into resilience has been his ultimate goal. This made him pursue his masters in the field of medical sociology, few months spent in the program have led to this wonderful book through the help of the Holy Ghost and my lecturers.